CliffsTestPrep®

Florida Real Estate Sales Associate Exam: 5 Practice Tests

by

John A. Yoegel, PhD, DREI, C-CREC

WILEY

Wiley Publishing, Inc.

About the Author

John Yoegel has been a real estate instructor for over 20 years and holds the Distinguished Real Estate Instructor designation from the Real Estate Educators Association.

Publisher's Acknowledgments

Editorial

Acquisitions Editor: Greg Tubach

Project Editor: Elizabeth Kuball

Technical Editor: Jack Bennett

Production

Proofreader: Vickie Broyles

Wiley Publishing, Inc. Composition Services

CliffsTestPrep® Florida Real Estate Sales Associate Exam: 5 Practice Tests

Published by:
Wiley Publishing, Inc.
111 River Street
Hoboken, NJ 07030-5774
www.wiley.com

Copyright © 2006 Wiley, Hoboken, NJ

Published by Wiley, Hoboken, NJ
Published simultaneously in Canada

Library of Congress Cataloging-in-Publication data is available from the publisher upon request.

ISBN-13: 978-0-470-03700-3

10 9 8 7 6 5 4 3 2 1

1O/SU/QY/QW/IN

WILEY

CliffsTestPrep®

Florida Real Estate Sales Associate Exam: 5 Practice Tests

Acknowledgments

I want to thank my wife, the lovely Marina, who has made so many of my endeavors, including this book, possible. Thanks also to my agent, Grace Freedson, who keeps me busy. I want to thank Acquisitions Editor Greg Tubach for getting me started on the right foot; Project Editor Elizabeth Kuball, who made this book considerably clearer for the readers; and Technical Editor Jack Bennett, who kept me on the straight and narrow with respect to the nuances of Florida real estate law and practice. I also wish to thank all of the students who through the years have put themselves in my hands. Sometimes I wonder who learned more, them or me.

Table of Contents

PART I: INTRODUCTION TO THE FLORIDA REAL ESTATE SALES ASSOCIATE EXAM

Introduction. 3
   How This Book Is Organized 3
   How to Use This Book 3
      Practice Taking a Typical Length Exam 4
      Practice Dealing with Various Types of Multiple-Choice Questions 4
      Review Important Subject Matter 5
      Self-Diagnose the Areas in Which You Need More Study. 5
      Develop Your Own Test-Taking Strategy. 6
   Getting Ready for Exam Day 7

PART II: PRACTICE TESTS

Practice Test 1 13

Answer Key 1 39
   Answer Key for Practice Test 1 39
   Answers and Explanations for Practice Test 1. 41

Practice Test 2 49

Answer Key 2 75
   Answer Key for Practice Test 2 75
   Answers and Explanations for Practice Test 2 77

Practice Test 3 85

Answer Key 3 111
   Answer Key for Practice Test 3 111
   Answers and Explanations for Practice Test 3. 113

Practice Test 4 121

Answer Key 4 147
   Answer Key for Practice Test 4 147
   Answers and Explanations for Practice Test 4 149

Practice Test 5 157

Answer Key 5 183
   Answer Key for Practice Test 5 183
   Answers and Explanations for Practice Test 5 185

Math Review 191
   Percentages 191
   Area and Volume 192
      Area of a Square or Rectangle. 193
      Area of a Triangle 194

Area of an Irregular Shape. 194
Volume of a Cube or Rectangular Solid 194
Volume of a Three-Dimensional Triangular Figure or a Pyramid. 195
Mortgage Calculations 197
Proration. 197
Appraisal and Valuation 198
Capitalization 198
Gross Multipliers. 199

PART I

INTRODUCTION TO THE FLORIDA REAL ESTATE SALES ASSOCIATE EXAM

Introduction

Thank you for purchasing CliffsTestPrep *Florida Real Estate Sales Associate Exam: 5 Practice Tests*. With this book, the material you learned in your courses and from your textbooks, and a little hard work, you'll be well prepared to take and pass the Florida exam and be on your way to a rewarding career in the real estate industry.

The principal purpose of this book is to provide you with practice tests to help you prepare for the state exam, so this introduction is brief. I know you're anxious to get to the practice tests, but I recommend starting by reviewing this introduction, as the material I cover here will help you get the maximum benefit from this book as well as offer some hints to help you do well on the state exam. Before you take your state exam, you may want to review the introduction again, particularly the information on exam taking hints.

I do want to make one note about what this book is *not* and how it should *not* be used. This is neither a textbook nor a reference book; it should be used only as a guide in passing your Florida real estate exam. To the extent possible, I tried to make the material current and correct in the context in which it is presented. The material is specifically designed around a multiple-choice testing format. As such, vital pieces of information that may change a particular circumstance in real life are often left out. Your ultimate real estate practice should be guided by your courses, your textbooks, and ultimately the brokers you work for, in order to maintain compliance with state law.

Although this book will give you practice for the state examination and will help you review the material on the exam, it is no substitute for study. Before tackling these practice tests, you should have a thorough knowledge of the material taught in your pre-licensing courses as well as the textbooks in the courses. You will also want to familiarize yourself with the information at the Florida Division of Real Estate (DRE) Web site (www.state.fl.us/dbpr/re/publications/frec/frec_syllabus.pdf), which has a great deal of information on exam content. You should also be familiar with the Candidate Information Booklet that can be obtained from the state at www.myflorida.com/dbpr/servop/testing/booklets/real/sl_bk.pdf. Once you feel you have a mastery of the necessary subject matter, begin taking the practice tests in this book.

How This Book Is Organized

The primary material in this book consists of five practice tests, each consisting of 100 multiple-choice questions with an answer key and explanations. The questions are typical of the type of questions that are asked on state real estate examinations. The content of the tests is designed to cover material as outlined at the State of Florida real estate licensing Web site.

How to Use This Book

I have attempted, in constructing the practice tests, to help you accomplish five goals:

- Practice taking a typical length exam
- Practice dealing with various types of multiple-choice questions
- Review important subject matter
- Self-diagnose the areas in which you need more study
- Develop your own test-taking style

In the following sections, I give you more information on each of these goals and show you how to accomplish them, keeping in mind that the ultimate goal is to help you pass the state exam.

Practice Taking a Typical Length Exam

The Florida Real Estate Sales Associate Exam consists of 100 multiple-choice questions. You have 3 hours and 30 minutes in which to complete the exam and you must score 75% (75 questions correct) in order to pass.

To use the tests in this book for practice, consider the following tips:

- Block out three and a half hours when you won't be interrupted.
- Plan on taking only one practice test at a sitting. These tests are fairly long and your best bet is to approach each one fresh.
- Find a quiet place where you won't be disturbed.
- Prepare your materials, including pencils and a calculator.
- Prepare a blank piece of paper with the numbers 1 to 100 on it so you won't mark up the book. Or, if you prefer, photocopy the pages in this book where you're supposed to mark your answers. This will allow you to take any of the exams a second time.
- When you take a practice test, make sure you keep track of your time. With exams of this length, tracking your time throughout the exam is important. You should try to complete about 33 questions per hour in order to finish in three hours and still have time for review.
- Correct the exam using the answer key and figure out your score.

Practice Dealing with Various Types of Multiple-Choice Questions

I have included several different types of multiple-choice questions in these tests in order to give you practice for the real thing.

The most common type of question is asked in a straightforward manner. This type of question is characterized by a statement, called the *stem*, that calls for picking a single answer from the four choices. The stem is generally constructed as a positive statement or question, such as, "Which of the following activities requires a real estate license?" or "Directions and distances are used in what type of system of legal description?"

The next type of question is asked in the negative and requires the selection of the single answer that does *not* fit into the group with the remaining answers, such as, "Which of the following activities does not require a real estate license?" The choices will consist of three activities that require a license and one (the correct answer) that does not. These questions are not necessarily more difficult than any other type of question, but after a series of straightforward questions asked in the positive, you need to be alert to the change in language. One way to handle this type of question is to change the stem to a positive statement and check each answer against that statement. In the example I'm using, you would rephrase the stem to read, "You need a real estate license to . . ." and then check each multiple-choice answer against that statement until you get to the one that doesn't need a license.

The third type of question is not really so much a different type of question as a different answer—"all of the above," "none of the above," "both A and B," and so on. There is no trick to answering these questions except knowing the material cold. These answers do, however, provide good study material in that the very nature of the question and answer provides a list of items to remember.

Math questions often create a great deal of anxiety among students and test takers. Once again, there is no substitute for studying and practice. A few cautions, however, are in order when approaching math questions. If you have any math anxiety or special difficulty with math problems, leave them for the end. Be sure to read the question carefully to see what is being asked. Make sure you don't leave out a step like converting from one unit of measure to another (for example, square feet to square yards). Finally, unlike other multiple-choice questions where your first answer is usually the correct one, work the math problem a second time to make sure you didn't copy down the wrong numbers or miss a step. (The incorrect answers in math questions are often answers that you would be likely to get if you made a common mistake, so double-checking your work ensures that you haven't arrived at one of the wrong answers.)

Some questions on the exam will be fact-based and others will be application-based. An example of this would be a question that involves prorating taxes at a closing. A fact-based question might ask who is charged for taxes on the day of closing. The answer is the buyer. An application-based question would actually give you the taxes and closing date and have you calculate the proration of the taxes. You'd have to know that the closing date is charged to the buyer in order to answer the question correctly. This exam-preparation book is heavily weighted toward fact-based questions, because if you've mastered the facts you can more readily apply them to application-based questions.

Review Important Subject Matter

I've constructed the questions and provided explanations along with the answers to allow you to go back over the questions and use them as a review. For example, any question where "all of the above" is the correct answer will provide you with a short list of items that you should study. There are a number of variations of different questions on the same topic among the tests. Although no test preparation book can guarantee that any particular topic will be on any specific exam, some subjects are typically covered. I've tried to make sure that these topics are adequately covered in various questions.

Self-Diagnose the Areas in Which You Need More Study

The way the practice tests in this book have been prepared will allow you to diagnose your weak areas so that you can concentrate your study time accordingly. The questions have been organized in groups according to the subject matter presented by the Florida Division of Real Estate. You can go to the Florida Division of Real Estate Web site at www. state.fl.us/dbpr/re/publications/frec/frec_syllabus.pdf to check out the various subjects. The following table gives you the question numbers in each of the practice tests relevant to each subject area.

Sections of the Exam	
Section	*Question Numbers on Practice Tests*
Administrative matters and course overview; the real estate business	1–4
Real estate license law and qualifications for licensure	5–9
Real estate license law and commission rules	10–13
Authorized relationships	14–19
Real estate brokerage activities: Guides for salespersons	20–23
Violations of license law, penalties, and procedures	24–27
Federal and state laws pertaining to real estate	28–32
Property rights: estates and tenancies; condominiums, cooperatives, and time-sharing	33–36
Titles, deeds, and ownership records	37–41
Legal descriptions	42–45
Real estate contracts	46–50
Real estate finance	51–54
Types of mortgages and sources of financing	55–59
Real-estate-related computation and closing of transactions	60–63
Real estate appraisal	64–68

(continued)

Sections of the Exam *(continued)*	
Section	*Question Numbers on Practice Tests*
Introduction to residential product knowledge	69–72
Real estate investments and business opportunity brokerage	73–77
Taxes affecting real estate	78–82
The real estate market	83–85
Planning and zoning	86–90
Real estate mathematics	91–100

After you take each exam, in addition to figuring out your total score, you should go back and see the number of questions in each area that you got right or wrong. By determining in which subjects you're the strongest and in which subjects you need more work, you can concentrate your study efforts on those areas in which you're weakest.

Ultimately, you should shoot for an overall score of 85% to 90% for the whole exam and no more than one question wrong in each subject area. This should give you a comfortable margin to pass the state exam.

Develop Your Own Test-Taking Strategy

There are several recommended strategies for taking multiple-choice tests in general and dealing with questions in particular. The five tests in this book will give you a chance to practice different approaches to test taking.

Although the suggested strategies are based on paper-and-pencil testing systems, many states, including Florida, have gone to a computerized test. To some extent, each of these strategies can be adapted to electronic, paperless testing systems.

The first approach is to go through the whole exam fairly quickly, answering the questions you know and skipping the ones you don't. Then go back and spend the remaining time answering those questions you skipped. If a question has you stumped, try to eliminate at least one or two answers you know to be wrong. If you can eliminate two answers, even if you have to guess, you've increased your odds to a 50-50 chance of guessing correctly. The thing you need to be careful about if you skip questions is keeping track of your place on the answer sheet. You'll have to do all this on scrap paper.

The second approach for taking the exam is just to go through each question in order. As I mention earlier, you'll have to keep good track of your time, making sure you don't spend too much time on any one question. It would be a shame to miss several questions that you know the answers to just because you ran out of time.

As for individual question strategies, assuming you have a good grasp of the material, your first instinct on a multiple-choice exam is generally correct. Don't overthink the questions or go back and second-guess yourself. Deal with the material in the question and don't let your imagination create "what if" circumstances that require you to change your answer. There are two exceptions to this advice:

- You should do the math questions twice if you have the time.
- If a later question (say, question 60) provides information that helps you get a better answer to an earlier question (say, question 20), then by all means use that new information and revise your answer.

Above all, read the questions and carefully note what they're asking for. Watch out for the "Which of the following is not . . ." question after a series of positive questions.

Getting Ready for Exam Day

You've studied the necessary material. You've taken each of the practice tests perhaps a few times, getting your score up to 85% or 90%. You're ready. Here are a few hints to get you successfully through the exam.

A few days or weeks before the state exam, find out exactly what you'll need to bring with you and find out what you *can't* bring with you. Permissible items change from time to time, so you need to check with the Florida Division of Real Estate or your course instructor on this. The rules for admission into the testing facility may also change from time to time, so check out the necessary procedures and requirements to take the exam.

Typically, you'll need some or all of the following items:

- **Calculator:** I always bring two just in case. Phone calculators or calculators in handheld data devices are prohibited.
- **Pencils:** You'll need pencils to work on your scrap paper. And as silly as it may sound, sharpen them at home because some testing centers do not have pencil sharpeners.
- **Identification:** A government-issued photo ID is required; a DMV card, driver's license, or passport will suffice.
- **Permit:** You may need some kind of permit to take the exam. Check out the procedure and make sure you have whatever the state sends you to let you into the exam.

Make sure you eat your regular meals before the exam. Don't eat anything too heavy or different from what you normally eat. If you have a medical condition that may require a snack during the period of the exam, get permission ahead of time in writing and bring it with you to the exam. DRE will allow hard candy—but usually not sandwiches or other food or drink items.

Don't bring anything with you that you won't need for the exam. Testing centers generally don't have places to safely put backpacks or briefcases and usually will not allow them into the exam room. Make sure not to bring your cell phone into the exam room; leave it at home or in your car trunk.

Prepare everything you'll need the night before and get a good night's sleep. Wake up in time to get to the testing center at least 15 to 30 minutes early and allow for traffic, finding a parking space, and mass-transit delays.

Finally, when you get to your seat, pay attention and follow the directions given to you by the exam proctor on using the computer. The proctors are there to assist you. When you're ready to go, sit back for a minute, take a breath (or two or three), and relax. You're prepared and you've practiced by taking the tests in this book.

Good luck and welcome to your new career!

PART II

PRACTICE TESTS

Answer Sheet for Practice Test 1

(Remove This Sheet and Use It to Mark Your Answers.)

1 Ⓐ Ⓑ Ⓒ Ⓓ	21 Ⓐ Ⓑ Ⓒ Ⓓ	41 Ⓐ Ⓑ Ⓒ Ⓓ
2 Ⓐ Ⓑ Ⓒ Ⓓ	22 Ⓐ Ⓑ Ⓒ Ⓓ	42 Ⓐ Ⓑ Ⓒ Ⓓ
3 Ⓐ Ⓑ Ⓒ Ⓓ	23 Ⓐ Ⓑ Ⓒ Ⓓ	43 Ⓐ Ⓑ Ⓒ Ⓓ
4 Ⓐ Ⓑ Ⓒ Ⓓ	24 Ⓐ Ⓑ Ⓒ Ⓓ	44 Ⓐ Ⓑ Ⓒ Ⓓ
5 Ⓐ Ⓑ Ⓒ Ⓓ	25 Ⓐ Ⓑ Ⓒ Ⓓ	45 Ⓐ Ⓑ Ⓒ Ⓓ
6 Ⓐ Ⓑ Ⓒ Ⓓ	26 Ⓐ Ⓑ Ⓒ Ⓓ	46 Ⓐ Ⓑ Ⓒ Ⓓ
7 Ⓐ Ⓑ Ⓒ Ⓓ	27 Ⓐ Ⓑ Ⓒ Ⓓ	47 Ⓐ Ⓑ Ⓒ Ⓓ
8 Ⓐ Ⓑ Ⓒ Ⓓ	28 Ⓐ Ⓑ Ⓒ Ⓓ	48 Ⓐ Ⓑ Ⓒ Ⓓ
9 Ⓐ Ⓑ Ⓒ Ⓓ	29 Ⓐ Ⓑ Ⓒ Ⓓ	49 Ⓐ Ⓑ Ⓒ Ⓓ
10 Ⓐ Ⓑ Ⓒ Ⓓ	30 Ⓐ Ⓑ Ⓒ Ⓓ	50 Ⓐ Ⓑ Ⓒ Ⓓ
11 Ⓐ Ⓑ Ⓒ Ⓓ	31 Ⓐ Ⓑ Ⓒ Ⓓ	51 Ⓐ Ⓑ Ⓒ Ⓓ
12 Ⓐ Ⓑ Ⓒ Ⓓ	32 Ⓐ Ⓑ Ⓒ Ⓓ	52 Ⓐ Ⓑ Ⓒ Ⓓ
13 Ⓐ Ⓑ Ⓒ Ⓓ	33 Ⓐ Ⓑ Ⓒ Ⓓ	53 Ⓐ Ⓑ Ⓒ Ⓓ
14 Ⓐ Ⓑ Ⓒ Ⓓ	34 Ⓐ Ⓑ Ⓒ Ⓓ	54 Ⓐ Ⓑ Ⓒ Ⓓ
15 Ⓐ Ⓑ Ⓒ Ⓓ	35 Ⓐ Ⓑ Ⓒ Ⓓ	55 Ⓐ Ⓑ Ⓒ Ⓓ
16 Ⓐ Ⓑ Ⓒ Ⓓ	36 Ⓐ Ⓑ Ⓒ Ⓓ	56 Ⓐ Ⓑ Ⓒ Ⓓ
17 Ⓐ Ⓑ Ⓒ Ⓓ	37 Ⓐ Ⓑ Ⓒ Ⓓ	57 Ⓐ Ⓑ Ⓒ Ⓓ
18 Ⓐ Ⓑ Ⓒ Ⓓ	38 Ⓐ Ⓑ Ⓒ Ⓓ	58 Ⓐ Ⓑ Ⓒ Ⓓ
19 Ⓐ Ⓑ Ⓒ Ⓓ	39 Ⓐ Ⓑ Ⓒ Ⓓ	59 Ⓐ Ⓑ Ⓒ Ⓓ
20 Ⓐ Ⓑ Ⓒ Ⓓ	40 Ⓐ Ⓑ Ⓒ Ⓓ	60 Ⓐ Ⓑ Ⓒ Ⓓ

61 Ⓐ Ⓑ Ⓒ Ⓓ	81 Ⓐ Ⓑ Ⓒ Ⓓ
62 Ⓐ Ⓑ Ⓒ Ⓓ	82 Ⓐ Ⓑ Ⓒ Ⓓ
63 Ⓐ Ⓑ Ⓒ Ⓓ	83 Ⓐ Ⓑ Ⓒ Ⓓ
64 Ⓐ Ⓑ Ⓒ Ⓓ	84 Ⓐ Ⓑ Ⓒ Ⓓ
65 Ⓐ Ⓑ Ⓒ Ⓓ	85 Ⓐ Ⓑ Ⓒ Ⓓ
66 Ⓐ Ⓑ Ⓒ Ⓓ	86 Ⓐ Ⓑ Ⓒ Ⓓ
67 Ⓐ Ⓑ Ⓒ Ⓓ	87 Ⓐ Ⓑ Ⓒ Ⓓ
68 Ⓐ Ⓑ Ⓒ Ⓓ	88 Ⓐ Ⓑ Ⓒ Ⓓ
69 Ⓐ Ⓑ Ⓒ Ⓓ	89 Ⓐ Ⓑ Ⓒ Ⓓ
70 Ⓐ Ⓑ Ⓒ Ⓓ	90 Ⓐ Ⓑ Ⓒ Ⓓ
71 Ⓐ Ⓑ Ⓒ Ⓓ	91 Ⓐ Ⓑ Ⓒ Ⓓ
72 Ⓐ Ⓑ Ⓒ Ⓓ	92 Ⓐ Ⓑ Ⓒ Ⓓ
73 Ⓐ Ⓑ Ⓒ Ⓓ	93 Ⓐ Ⓑ Ⓒ Ⓓ
74 Ⓐ Ⓑ Ⓒ Ⓓ	94 Ⓐ Ⓑ Ⓒ Ⓓ
75 Ⓐ Ⓑ Ⓒ Ⓓ	95 Ⓐ Ⓑ Ⓒ Ⓓ
76 Ⓐ Ⓑ Ⓒ Ⓓ	96 Ⓐ Ⓑ Ⓒ Ⓓ
77 Ⓐ Ⓑ Ⓒ Ⓓ	97 Ⓐ Ⓑ Ⓒ Ⓓ
78 Ⓐ Ⓑ Ⓒ Ⓓ	98 Ⓐ Ⓑ Ⓒ Ⓓ
79 Ⓐ Ⓑ Ⓒ Ⓓ	99 Ⓐ Ⓑ Ⓒ Ⓓ
80 Ⓐ Ⓑ Ⓒ Ⓓ	100 Ⓐ Ⓑ Ⓒ Ⓓ

CUT HERE

CUT HERE

Practice Test 1

Directions: For each of the following questions, select the choice that best answers the question.

1. The property management field has experienced recent growth primarily due to an increase in

   A. the number of investment properties.
   B. the returns on investment properties.
   C. the number of absentee owners.
   D. interest rates.

2. The geographic area that a real estate broker or sales associate specializes in is called the

   A. market segment.
   B. specialty area.
   C. listing area.
   D. farm area.

3. A unique aspect of business brokerage as opposed to real estate brokerage is the broker's ability to

   A. locate buyers.
   B. write appropriate advertising.
   C. place a value on goodwill.
   D. locate sellers.

4. Which of the following is not considered residential property?

   A. one- to four-family house
   B. vacant land zoned for four families or fewer
   C. agricultural property of 10 or fewer acres
   D. apartment houses with fewer than ten units

GO ON TO THE NEXT PAGE

5. A person who wants to have a broker's license but does not want to operate her own office would likely become a

    A. sales associate.

    B. sales agent.

    C. assistant broker.

    D. broker associate.

6. Which of the following is not required background information on a real estate license application?

    A. pled nolo contendere to a crime

    B. convicted of a crime

    C. pled guilty to a crime

    D. proof of U.S. citizenship

7. What is the length of residency necessary to be considered a Florida resident for real estate licensing purposes?

    A. one year

    B. six months

    C. four months

    D. one month

8. Which of the following real estate activities does not require a real estate license?

    A. selling cemetery lots

    B. auctioning a single-family house

    C. exchanging a commercial office building

    D. leasing a store in a mall

9. Whether a real estate license holder from another state can obtain a Florida real estate license will depend on

   A. nondisclosure agreements.
   B. agency rules in the person's home state.
   C. mutual recognition agreements.
   D. residency rules.

10. The Florida Real Estate Commission is administratively part of the

    A. Florida Department of Consumer Protection.
    B. Florida Department of Education.
    C. Florida Department of Business and Professional Regulation.
    D. Florida Association of Realtors.

11. Which of the following is not a function or Purpose of the Florida Real Estate Commission?

    A. to protect the public
    B. to regulate proprietary real estate schools
    C. to regulate college real estate courses
    D. to limit broker and sales associate liability

12. What is the minimum number of brokers who have five years or more experience required to be on the Florida Real Estate Commission?

    A. two
    B. three
    C. four
    D. five

GO ON TO THE NEXT PAGE

13. Florida Real Estate Commission members are

A. elected.
B. appointed by the state senate.
C. appointed by the State Association of Realtors.
D. appointed by the governor.

14. A typical relationship of a real estate broker to a principal in a real estate sales transaction is as a

A. principal agent.
B. universal agent.
C. general agent.
D. special agent.

15. The best term used to describe the relationship of trust between a broker and a buyer or a broker and a seller in a single agency relationship is a

A. representational relationship.
B. fiduciary relationship.
C. customer relationship.
D. principal relationship.

16. The duty of a broker in a single agent relationship to represent the interests of her client even above her own interests is a result of the obligation of

A. obedience.
B. loyalty.
C. skill and care.
D. confidentiality.

17. Which of the following is not true about a designated sales associate agency arrangement?

  A. The broker acts as an agent to only one party.
  B. It must be a nonresidential transaction.
  C. The buyer and seller must have assets of $1 million or more.
  D. Both the buyer and the seller must request this relationship.

18. A broker transitioning from a single agent relationship to a transactional brokerage status

  A. must file appropriate documentation with the state.
  B. can do so with no special permission other than informing the parties.
  C. is illegal.
  D. can be done only with the principal's consent.

19. If a customer or principal refuses to sign an agency disclosure document, the agent must

  A. refuse the listing.
  B. refuse to represent the buyer.
  C. note the refusal in the file with the disclosure document.
  D. file a separate affidavit of disclosure with the state.

20. A real estate broker placed the following advertisement in a newspaper: "Three-bedroom house for sale. Call 555-5555." This is an example of a(n)

  A. false advertisement.
  B. acceptable advertisement.
  C. blind advertisement.
  D. fraudulent advertisement.

GO ON TO THE NEXT PAGE

21. If a broker places the names of her sales associates on her office sign, what else must she put on the sign for each associate?

    A. phone number
    B. license status
    C. years with the firm
    D. years licensed

22. A Florida real estate broker who calls an owner whose property is listed for sale as a for sale by owner (FSBO) and whose phone number appears on the yard sign

    A. is exempt from federal do-not-call laws.
    B. can do so for up to 18 months after the sign first appears.
    C. can do so for up to a year if the FSBO previously asked the broker for information.
    D. is in violation of federal do-not-call laws.

23. A sales associate who advertises real estate services in her own name

    A. is violating no law.
    B. can do so only with her supervising broker's permission.
    C. can do so on giveaways like calendars but not on sales brochures.
    D. cannot do so without including the broker's name.

24. An alleged violation of the real estate license law is a good definition of a

    A. fraud.
    B. complaint.
    C. final order.
    D. probable cause.

25. The maximum number of years for which a real estate license may be suspended by Florida state authorities is

    A. ten.

    B. five.

    C. three.

    D. one.

26. The Florida Real Estate Recovery Fund was created to reimburse

    A. monetary damages only.

    B. punitive damages only.

    C. monetary and punitive damages.

    D. none of the above

27. If a complainant withdraws his complaint against a real estate license after having filed it, which of the following is true?

    A. The investigation automatically stops.

    B. The investigation of the complaint will continue.

    C. The investigation will continue if the violation occurred within the last six months.

    D. The investigation may continue.

28. The 1866 Civil Rights Act is unique because

    A. it deals only with race and gender discrimination.

    B. it has no exceptions.

    C. complaints are made to HUD.

    D. all of the above

GO ON TO THE NEXT PAGE

29. Which of the following is not covered by the Federal Fair Housing Act?

    A. owner-occupied single-family house

    B. single-family house owned by the government

    C. six-unit multifamily building

    D. four single-family houses owned by the same person

30. The owner of a six-unit apartment house has ten years of research indicating levels of wear and tear on the apartments by different groups of people such as different ethnic groups, age groups, and people with children. Based on his research, he charges different security deposits to these different groups. This practice is

    A. acceptable as long as he has the research to back it up.

    B. acceptable for the families with children but not for the ethnic or age groups.

    C. acceptable under federal law regardless of the research.

    D. illegal.

31. Which of the following primarily concerns itself with advertising with respect to credit terms?

    A. Truth in Lending Act

    B. Real Estate Settlement and Procedures Act

    C. Florida Fair Lending Act

    D. Equal Credit Opportunity Act

32. The Florida Uniform Lands Sales Practices Act requires registration of subdivisions of

    A. 10 or more lots.

    B. 25 or more lots.

    C. 40 or more lots.

    D. 50 or more lots.

33. Real property can also be described as

   A. personal property.
   B. the bundle of rights.
   C. chattels.
   D. land.

34. The rights of a landowner to a river bordering her property are known as

   A. littoral rights.
   B. correlative use rights.
   C. riparian rights.
   D. rights of appropriation.

35. In the case of a transfer of ownership of a piece of real estate, a fixture is normally

   A. assumed to be included in the transfer.
   B. assumed to remain with the original owner.
   C. transferred only if there is an agreement.
   D. subject to a separate bill of sale.

36. A tenant who operates a jewelry store wants to take his jewelry cases with him at the expiration of the lease. Which of the following is most correct?

   A. He may take the jewelry cases.
   B. He may not take the jewelry cases.
   C. He may take the cases only if he has a prior agreement with the landlord.
   D. He may take the cases if removal will not cause substantial damage.

GO ON TO THE NEXT PAGE

37. All liens are encumbrances. All encumbrances are

    A. liens.
    B. limitations.
    C. voluntary.
    D. involuntary.

38. A construction lien creates

    A. a cloud on title.
    B. a marketable title.
    C. a transferable title.
    D. no problem in transferring title.

39. A deed restriction prohibiting the sale of property to certain ethnic groups

    A. is enforceable only if the restriction predates civil rights laws.
    B. is enforceable in subdivisions of fewer than five lots.
    C. supersedes civil rights laws.
    D. is illegal and unenforceable.

40. The process by which eminent domain occurs is called

    A. alienation.
    B. inverse condemnation.
    C. police power.
    D. condemnation.

41. Owner A sells a piece of his property to Buyer B. In order for Owner A to get access to the county road from the portion of land he still owns, he needs an easement across Buyer B's property. In order to accomplish this, which of the following has to occur?

   A. Owner A must grant an easement appurtenant to Buyer B.

   B. Owner A must grant an easement in gross to Buyer B.

   C. Owner A must reserve an easement in gross for himself.

   D. Owner A must reserve an easement appurtenant for himself.

42. A legal description of property is not adequate unless

   A. a street address is included.

   B. at least two different methods are used.

   C. it includes a detailed description of the structures.

   D. none of the above

43. The lot and block system of property description is not also known as the

   A. lot, block, and tract system.

   B. subdivision system.

   C. rectangular survey system.

   D. plat map system.

44. How many acres does a section of land contain?

   A. 40

   B. 160

   C. 320

   D. 640

GO ON TO THE NEXT PAGE

45. A surveyor whom you hire mentions terms like *baselines* and *meridians* when surveying your property. What system of legal description is he most likely using?

    A. government survey

    B. metes and bounds

    C. Spanish land grant

    D. lot and block

46. The statute of limitations for contracts in Florida is

    A. five years for oral and written contracts.

    B. four years for oral and written contracts.

    C. four years for oral contracts and five years for written contracts.

    D. four years for written contracts and five years for oral contracts.

47. One party agrees to sell another party a piece of property in exchange for a certain amount of money. The agreement is in writing. What type of contract do the parties have?

    A. express bilateral

    B. express unilateral

    C. implied bilateral

    D. implied unilateral

48. Owner A hires someone to burn down his building for the insurance money. They agree on all the terms including payment. The contract would be

    A. valid.

    B. void.

    C. voidable.

    D. unenforceable.

49. An option to purchase property is considered an

   A. express bilateral agreement.
   B. express unilateral agreement.
   C. implied bilateral agreement.
   D. implied unilateral agreement.

50. In an option agreement, the consideration is

   A. the amount to be paid for the property.
   B. 10% of the amount to be paid for the property.
   C. the amount paid for the right to purchase the property.
   D. usually refundable if the option is not exercised.

51. Florida operates under the idea that a borrower in a mortgage loan situation retains title to the property. This is known as the

   A. mortgage theory.
   B. lien theory.
   C. title theory.
   D. promissory note theory.

52. The terms and conditions of the promise to pay back money borrowed to buy a house is found in the

   A. mortgage.
   B. trust deed.
   C. promissory note.
   D. deed of trust.

GO ON TO THE NEXT PAGE

53. The process by which a mortgage loan is paid off in equal payments consisting of principal and interest is called

  A. discounting.
  B. amortization.
  C. a term loan.
  D. an equity loan.

54. What does a discount point do to the effective yield that a lender gets from a mortgage loan?

  A. It raises it.
  B. It has no effect.
  C. It lowers it.
  D. It lowers it, but only if the seller—not the buyer—pays it.

55. Equity is most accurately defined as the

  A. sale price of the house minus the mortgage amount.
  B. value of the house minus all liens and encumbrances.
  C. value of the house minus the mortgage.
  D. amount of the down payment.

56. A mortgage lender requires a borrower to make monthly payments—in addition to the mortgage payments—to a special account to cover taxes and hazard insurance costs for the property. This type of account is commonly called a(n)

  A. savings account.
  B. tax account.
  C. impound account.
  D. takeout account.

57. A type of purchase financing that allows the seller to take immediate possession of the property but delays transfer of title is

   A. a land contract.

   B. a contract for deed.

   C. an installment sales contract.

   D. all of the above

58. The interest rate charged by the Federal Reserve System to borrow money is called the

   A. open market rate.

   B. prime rate.

   C. discount rate.

   D. reserve rate.

59. Buyer A borrows money to buy a house. As part of the repayment plan, when he sells the house he will have to turn over a portion of the profit he makes on the house to the lender. This type of mortgage is called a

   A. shared appreciation mortgage.

   B. graduated payment mortgage.

   C. reverse annuity mortgage.

   D. growing equity mortgage.

60. How does the total purchase price appear in a closing statement?

   A. credit to seller; debit to buyer

   B. credit to seller; credit to buyer

   C. debit to buyer; debit to seller

   D. debit to seller; credit to buyer

GO ON TO THE NEXT PAGE

61. According to the buyer's closing statement, the buyer must pay

  A. all debits.
  B. all credits.
  C. all debits plus all credits.
  D. the difference between all credits and all debits.

62. Which of the following is true about items to be paid at closing, including prorated items?

  A. The amounts are fixed by Florida state law.
  B. Who pays each item is fixed by Florida state law.
  C. Who pays each item is fixed by federal law.
  D. All charges are negotiable.

63. Which of the following is not a typical way to calculate prorations?

  A. statutory month method
  B. statutory year method
  C. 365-day-year method
  D. 365-day-year/30-day-month method

64. According to Florida state law, a licensed broker

  A. may not do an appraisal.
  B. may only do a CMA.
  C. may do both a CMA and an appraisal.
  D. who is doing an appraisal is exempt from the USPAP.

65. The most profitable single use that will generate the highest value for a piece of property is called its

    A. economical use.
    B. feasible use.
    C. highest and best use.
    D. anticipated use.

66. Which of the following is not a characteristic of value?

    A. change
    B. utility
    C. transferability
    D. demand

67. Two lots, each valued at $50,000, when combined have a value of $125,000. What term best describes this added value?

    A. supply and demand
    B. substitution
    C. utility
    D. plottage

68. In appraising a property, the process by which dissimilarities are accounted for in comparing a subject property and a comparable property is called

    A. reconciling the values.
    B. making adjustments.
    C. equalization.
    D. estimating value.

GO ON TO THE NEXT PAGE

69. The primary purpose of a building code is to

    A.   insure that homes are built to current architectural standards.

    B.   guarantee a comfortable environment to the occupants.

    C.   insure that property values are maintained.

    D.   insure that structures are safe and sanitary.

70. A framing type often associated with stucco-covered houses in order to minimize cracking is

    A.   platform framing.

    B.   balloon framing.

    C.   timber framing.

    D.   precut framing.

71. Which is likely to be the most private of the following lot types?

    A.   key lot

    B.   T intersection lot

    C.   interior lot

    D.   cul-de-sac lot

72. The effectiveness of insulation is measured by

    A.   width in inches.

    B.   R factor.

    C.   BTUs.

    D.   SEER.

73. All of the following are considered advantages in investing in real estate except

- **A.** use of leverage.
- **B.** liquidity.
- **C.** tax advantages.
- **D.** high rates of return.

74. The importance of location and the fact that real estate is immobile cause all real estate markets to be

- **A.** low risk.
- **B.** highly leveraged.
- **C.** local in nature.
- **D.** equally risky.

75. The difference between the value of a property and all debts associated with it is a good definition of

- **A.** leverage.
- **B.** equity.
- **C.** return.
- **D.** appreciation.

76. The method of appraising a business that converts an anticipated income stream to a present value is called the

- **A.** reproduction cost minus depreciation approach.
- **B.** income capitalization approach.
- **C.** comparable sales approach.
- **D.** liquidation analysis.

GO ON TO THE NEXT PAGE

77. The total value of an established business that may differ from the value of the business's physical assets is known as the

    A. going concern value.
    B. good will value.
    C. value in use.
    D. investment value.

78. The term *ad valorem* is most closely associated with

    A. appraised value.
    B. market value.
    C. assessed value.
    D. investment value.

79. The tax year in Florida for local property taxes is

    A. June 1 to May 31.
    B. July 1 to June 30.
    C. January 1 to December 31.
    D. April 15 to April 14.

80. The final step in protesting a tax assessment is

    A. an appeal to the tax assessor.
    B. a petition to the value adjustment board.
    C. an appeal to the city or town council.
    D. litigation in the courts.

81. Which of the following is most nearly correct as the way a municipality determines the tax rate?

    A. Total Budget ÷ Total Assessed Value

    B. Total Budget × Assessed Value

    C. Total budget ÷ Total Number of Nonexempt Properties

    D. Total Budget ÷ Average Assessed Value

82. Which of the following is not a way to eliminate, decrease, or defer capital gains on a real estate transaction?

    A. like kind exchange

    B. all cash sale

    C. installment sale

    D. none of the above

83. Which of the following would not be considered a household?

    A. a single person living in a rented apartment

    B. a couple living with one of their parents

    C. a single mother with two children living in their own home

    D. a widower living in a rented apartment

84. Which of the following is primarily responsible for determining the value of a property?

    A. buyer

    B. seller

    C. appraiser

    D. real estate agent

GO ON TO THE NEXT PAGE

85. The fact that the value of a piece of property is influenced by what goes on around it is a function of the property's

A. uniqueness.

B. indestructibility.

C. supply.

D. immobility.

86. A statement of the goals and policies regarding growth of a community is a good definition of the

A. zoning ordinance.

B. general plan.

C. specific plan.

D. subdivision regulations.

87. The proper way for a landowner who has physical difficulty in developing his property to get relief is to obtain a

A. rezoning.

B. conditional use permit.

C. master plan amendment.

D. variance.

88. What is the study of population characteristics called?

A. demography

B. anthropology

C. sociology

D. urban planning

89. Owner A owns 10 acres on which there is a deed restriction prohibiting subdivision of the land into smaller parcels. The local zoning permits homes to be built on parcels of 2 acres or more. Which of the following is true?

   A. Owner A may subdivide his land.
   B. Owner A may not subdivide his land.
   C. The land may only be subdivided if Owner A sells the property in order to eliminate the deed restriction.
   D. Owner A may subdivide the land but must sell the properties with the same deed restrictions in place.

90. The adoption and enforcement of zoning laws is an exercise of what type of power by the local government?

   A. the police power
   B. the eminent domain law
   C. the law of escheat
   D. the subdivision laws

91. A person who wants to buy a $200,000 home by putting down $40,000 in cash and borrowing $160,000 is making use of what financial concept?

   A. leverage
   B. equity yield
   C. total yield
   D. discount rate

92. A home buyer borrows $280,000 to purchase a home for 30 years at an interest rate of 7%. How much interest will he pay the first year on an interest-only loan?

   A. $19,600
   B. $5,599
   C. $1,634
   D. Not enough information is provided.

GO ON TO THE NEXT PAGE

93. A purchaser wants to buy a house that costs $330,000. The bank is offering a mortgage loan at a loan-to-value ratio of 80%. How much will the purchaser need for a down payment?

    A. $330,000

    B. $264,000

    C. $66,000

    D. $33,000

94. Buyer A pays $300,000 for a house, putting down $60,000 and borrowing $240,000. The house appreciates 25% during the years he owns it. When he sells the house, what is his profit?

    A. $15,000

    B. $75,000

    C. $135,000

    D. $375,000

95. A seller has paid taxes of $3,650 in arrears on November 15 for that year (January 1–December 31). The closing is on December 1. Who owes how much to whom?

    A. The seller owes the buyer $310.

    B. The buyer owes the seller $310.

    C. The seller owes the buyer $3,340.

    D. The buyer owes the seller $3,340.

96. What is the commission on the sale of a house that sold for $475,000 if the commission rate was 5%?

    A. $23,750

    B. $21,675

    C. $18,450

    D. $11,250

97. A buyer agrees to buy a property for $425,000. It is appraised at $400,000. The bank is offering a mortgage loan at a loan-to-value ratio of 80%. How much of a down payment will be necessary to purchase this property?

    A. $340,000

    B. $70,000

    C. $80,000

    D. $105,000

98. A seller pays $13,500 in commission. At a commission rate of 5.5%, how much did the house sell for?

    A. $213,670

    B. $227,450

    C. $236,560

    D. $245,455

99. How much will the documentary stamp tax be on a property that sold outside Dade County for $403,500?

    A. $4,035.00

    B. $2,824.50

    C. $2,421.00

    D. $282.45

100. What would the state intangible tax be on a previously recorded mortgage in the amount of $130,000 that is assumed by a buyer?

    A. $0

    B. $260

    C. $2,600

    D. Not enough information is provided.

Answer Key 1

Answer Key for Practice Test 1

1. C		**31.** A	
2. D		**32.** D	
3. C		**33.** B	
4. D		**34.** C	
5. D		**35.** A	
6. D		**36.** D	
7. C		**37.** B	
8. A		**38.** A	
9. C		**39.** D	
10. C		**40.** D	
11. D		**41.** D	
12. C		**42.** D	
13. D		**43.** C	
14. D		**44.** D	
15. B		**45.** A	
16. B		**46.** C	
17. A		**47.** A	
18. D		**48.** B	
19. C		**49.** B	
20. C		**50.** C	
21. B		**51.** B	
22. D		**52.** C	
23. D		**53.** B	
24. B		**54.** A	
25. A		**55.** B	
26. A		**56.** C	
27. D		**57.** D	
28. B		**58.** C	
29. A		**59.** A	
30. D		**60.** A	

61. D		**81.** A	
62. D		**82.** B	
63. D		**83.** B	
64. C		**84.** A	
65. C		**85.** D	
66. A		**86.** B	
67. D		**87.** D	
68. B		**88.** A	
69. D		**89.** B	
70. B		**90.** A	
71. D		**91.** A	
72. B		**92.** A	
73. B		**93.** C	
74. C		**94.** B	
75. B		**95.** B.	
76. B		**96.** A	
77. A		**97.** D	
78. C		**98.** D	
79. C		**99.** B	
80. D		**100.** A	

Answers and Explanations for Practice Test 1

1. C. Increase in absentee owners has increased the need for property managers.

2. D. This is an industry term for a geographic area in which a broker or sales associate concentrates his efforts.

3. C. The other tasks are all necessary in any type of real estate or business brokerage.

4. D. This is definitional.

5. D. The broker associate license (formerly broker salesperson license) allows a person to have a broker's license but work under the supervision of another broker.

6. D. U.S. citizenship is not required.

7. C. This is statutory.

8. A. This is statutory. *Note:* Questions are often written with very little information. Be careful not to overthink a question or bring in extraneous information not present in the question. For example, in this question, all of the answers would be correct—that is, exempt—if the individual were dealing with her own property.

9. C. The other answers have no bearing on whether or not a licensed nonresident can get a Florida license.

10. C. This is statutory.

11. D. The selected items are statutorily, among other things, the purpose and function of the committee.

12. C. This is statutory.

13. D. They are appointed by the governor and confirmed by the state senate.

14. D. A real estate agent is usually authorized to represent the principal in one transaction. That is the definition of a special agent. There is no such thing as a principal agent.

15. B. This is definitional.

16. B. The other choices are also part of the duties owed to a client, but loyalty requires putting the client's interest above all others.

17. A. The broker acts in a neutral capacity as an advisor to both sales associates.

18. D. This is statutory.

19. C. There is no separate affidavit. The listing agreement will have a place for the principal to sign acknowledging agency disclosure, so Choice A is usually not an issue.

20. C. Advertisements by real estate licensees should clearly identify the fact that the public (the reader of the ad) is dealing with a real estate licensee.

21. B. The law requires that if associates' names are placed on the sign, their status as broker associates or sales associates must be placed next to their names.

22. D. Choice C may be a little tricky. A broker may call a FSBO for up to three months if the owner had previously made an inquiry to the broker.

23. D. This is statutory.

24. B. This is definitional. Filing the complaint is the first step in the complaint process.

25. A. This is statutory.

26. A. This is statutory. Monetary damages are also referred to as compensatory damages.

27. D. The investigation may continue at the discretion of the state. This answer is more correct than Choice B, which states that the investigation will continue.

28. B. There are no exceptions to this law.

29. A. This is statutory.

30. D. Changing the terms or conditions of a rental for different protected classes is illegal.

31. A. Although all of the laws mentioned involve mortgage lending practices, truth in lending concerns itself with, among other things, advertising of loan information.

32. D. This is statutory.

33. B. Choices A and C are definitely wrong, because *chattel* is another term for personal property. The term *land* is usually used to describe the physical surface of the Earth and all that it comprises, including minerals and soil; it is not used to describe the rights of ownership.

34. C. Littoral rights refer to still bodies of water. The right of appropriation has to do with state rights, and correlative use relates to underground water use.

35. A. A fixture is normally included in the transfer of ownership unless there is an agreement to the contrary.

36. D. This is the most correct choice, given the information. Trade fixtures normally belong to the tenant and may be removed unless otherwise stated in the lease, but the damage must not be substantial and must be able to be easily repaired.

37. B. Choice B is the only completely true statement. All encumbrances are some form of limitation on title or property use.

38. A. All liens tend to create clouds on titles, some more easily resolved than others.

39. D. The object of a deed restriction must be legal.

40. D. The police power grants the government the right of eminent domain, but the process by which it is implemented is called *condemnation.*

41. D. Because this easement attaches itself to Owner A's land, it is an easement appurtenant so choices B and C are incorrect. An owner selling property and needing to retain an easement across the property sold reserves an easement.

42. D. A street address may not be available for rural properties. One method is sufficient, though sometimes two methods are combined. Legal descriptions define land boundaries, so specific structures are not part of the description.

43. C. The rectangular survey system is a different system of legal description.

44. D. This is something you'll have to memorize.

45. A. These terms are only associated with the government or rectangular survey system.

46. C. This is statutory.

47. A. The fact that it is in writing makes this an express contract, and both parties having agreed to act makes this a bilateral agreement.

48. B. The contract is not valid and, therefore, is void because the object of the contract—that is, burning down the building—is illegal.

49. B. Because it's a real estate agreement, it will be in writing—therefore, express—and only one party must act, so it is unilateral.

50. C. The consideration is paid to obtain the right to purchase property at some future date. It is not refundable.

51. B. This is definitional and means that the mortgage holder (the lender) has a lien on the property.

52. C. Choices A, B, and D all relate to the document using the property as security for the note but not the terms of the note itself.

53. B. Amortization results in the loan being paid off gradually over time.

54. **A.** Discount points raise the yield to the lender above that of the stated interest rate, so if points were paid to secure a 6% loan, the yield to the bank would be more than 6%. How much more depends on how many points are paid.

55. **B.** Although, at the moment of sale, if the sale price equals the value, choices A and D would be correct, the most accurate choice is B.

56. **C.** This is definitional. The other answer choices are made up.

57. **D.** Choices A, B, and C are different names for the same purchase finance arrangement.

58. **C.** This is definitional.

59. **A.** The shared appreciation mortgage requires some of the profit made when selling the house to be shared with the lender.

60. **A.** Since the buyer will pay and the seller is owed the purchase price, it is charged as a credit to the seller and a debit to the buyer.

61. **D.** Credits either have already been paid or are owed to the buyer. Debits are what remain to be paid. So the buyer owes the difference between the two numbers.

62. **D.** This is statutory, although if the items are not negotiated, there are statutes as well as common practice that govern who pays what.

63. **D.** Choices A and B are really variations of the same method. Choice D is mathematically impossible.

64. **C.** A licensed broker or sales associate may do a comparative market analysis or an appraisal. The appraisal must meet Uniform Standards of Professional Appraisal Practice (USPAP).

65. **C.** The highest and best use is that use the property can be put to that will result in its highest value.

66. **A.** Change is a principle of value, not a characteristic of value. The fourth characteristic of value is scarcity.

67. **D.** Two or more properties when combined may benefit from the increase in size, which allows more varied uses. This increase in value is called *plottage*.

68. **B.** Adjusting comparables to the subject is the process of accounting for differences between properties. Reconciling comes near the end of the appraisal process. *Equalization* is a term associated with tax assessment. Estimating value is the definition of appraising.

69. **D.** Building codes may indirectly accomplish some of the other choices, but the primary purpose is to maintain safe and sanitary structures within a community.

70. **B.** Balloon framing uses continuous studs from the foundation to the ceiling of the second floor.

71. **D.** The interior lot has other lots on two sides. The cul-de-sac lot is often larger and has less traffic than the other lots.

72. **B.** The R factor is the measure for the efficiency and effectiveness of insulation because it takes into account the various efficiencies of different types of insulation to reduce heat loss.

73. **B.** Real estate is generally considered to be an illiquid investment that is not readily sold.

74. **C.** The characteristics described—location and immobility—make all real estate markets local in character.

75. **B.** This is a little tricky because overall value is used in some of the calculations for appreciation and the use of borrowed funds (leverage). But the definition in the question is the exact definition of equity (that is, the owner's share of the property after all debts are accounted for).

76. **B.** This is definitional. This approach makes use of a capitalization rate to convert income into value.

77. **A.** This is definitional. Choice B is sometimes part of a total business value. Choices C and D are types of real estate value.

78. **C.** Although market value and appraised value (not investment value) could form the basis for assessed value, the term *ad valorem* deals with property taxes, which are based on assessed value.

79. C. This is statutory.

80. D. This is statutory. Choices A and B are the first two steps, respectively. Choice D is not an option.

81. A. This is statutory. More precisely the formula is:

(Approved Budget – Non-Property-Tax Revenue) ÷ (Total Assessed Value – Exemptions)

82. B. Choices A and C will defer or decrease capital gains tax. Cash sale would not.

83. B. The definition of a household revolves around living in a separate dwelling unit rather than whether a person is single, married, or has children.

84. A. The only choice that may trip you up here is Choice C, appraiser. Remember that an appraiser estimates value based on the market; an appraiser does not determine value.

85. D. Because property cannot be moved, it is affected by what happens around it.

86. B. All of the incorrect answers control and guide growth in some way, but the general statement of policies and goals for a community is contained in the general plan, also called the master plan.

87. D. Where the owner of a single lot has practical difficulty in developing that lot, a variance is most appropriate.

88. A. This is definitional.

89. B. The rule is that if a deed restriction and local laws conflict, the stricter rule will apply. In this case, the deed restriction is stricter than the local zoning.

90. A. This is statutory.

91. A. Using other people's (borrowed) money to extend the buying power of your own money is called *leveraging*.

92. A. Interest on a mortgage loan is calculated this way:

Total Amount Borrowed × Interest Rate = Interest Paid

$280,000 × 0.07 = $19,600

93. C. The percent quoted as the loan-to-value (LTV) ratio is the amount the bank will lend. The remainder is what is needed for the down payment.

100% (purchase price) – 80% (LTV) = 20% (down payment)

$330,000 (purchase price) × 0.20 (down payment) = $66,000 (cash needed)

94. B. Profit is calculated by multiplying the rate of appreciation by the total price of the house.

$300,000 × 0.25 = $75,000

95. B. The seller will have been in the house for all but 31 days of the year, December having 31 days and the closing date belonging to the buyer. Because the seller paid for the entire year, the buyer will owe the seller for the 31 days of December.

$3,650 ÷ 365 = $10 per day

$10 × 31 = $310 buyer owes to seller

96. A. The formula is:

Sales Price × Commission Rate = Commission

$475,000 × 0.05 = $23,750

97. D. This problem is less about the math than it is about remembering that banks make mortgage loans based on appraised value.

$400,000 (appraised value) × 0.80 (LTV) = $320,000 (mortgage loan)

$425,000 (sale price) – $320,000 (mortgage loan) = $105,000 (down payment)

98. D. The formula is:

Commission Amount ÷ Commission Rate = Sale Price

$13,500 ÷ 0.055 (commission rate) = $245,455 (rounded)

Note: Don't worry about rounding on the exam. Exam writers will not give you choices that are right or wrong based on small rounding issues.

99. B. Documentary stamps are charged at the rate of $0.70 per $100 of sale price, except in Dade County, where the fee is $0.60 per $100.

$403,500 ÷ $100 = 4,035 units (each of which is taxed at $0.70)

4,035 units × $0.70 = $2,824.50

100. A. No state intangible tax is due on previously recorded mortgages if they're assumed.

Answer Sheet for Practice Test 2

(Remove This Sheet and Use It to Mark Your Answers.)

1 Ⓐ Ⓑ Ⓒ Ⓓ	21 Ⓐ Ⓑ Ⓒ Ⓓ	41 Ⓐ Ⓑ Ⓒ Ⓓ
2 Ⓐ Ⓑ Ⓒ Ⓓ	22 Ⓐ Ⓑ Ⓒ Ⓓ	42 Ⓐ Ⓑ Ⓒ Ⓓ
3 Ⓐ Ⓑ Ⓒ Ⓓ	23 Ⓐ Ⓑ Ⓒ Ⓓ	43 Ⓐ Ⓑ Ⓒ Ⓓ
4 Ⓐ Ⓑ Ⓒ Ⓓ	24 Ⓐ Ⓑ Ⓒ Ⓓ	44 Ⓐ Ⓑ Ⓒ Ⓓ
5 Ⓐ Ⓑ Ⓒ Ⓓ	25 Ⓐ Ⓑ Ⓒ Ⓓ	45 Ⓐ Ⓑ Ⓒ Ⓓ
6 Ⓐ Ⓑ Ⓒ Ⓓ	26 Ⓐ Ⓑ Ⓒ Ⓓ	46 Ⓐ Ⓑ Ⓒ Ⓓ
7 Ⓐ Ⓑ Ⓒ Ⓓ	27 Ⓐ Ⓑ Ⓒ Ⓓ	47 Ⓐ Ⓑ Ⓒ Ⓓ
8 Ⓐ Ⓑ Ⓒ Ⓓ	28 Ⓐ Ⓑ Ⓒ Ⓓ	48 Ⓐ Ⓑ Ⓒ Ⓓ
9 Ⓐ Ⓑ Ⓒ Ⓓ	29 Ⓐ Ⓑ Ⓒ Ⓓ	49 Ⓐ Ⓑ Ⓒ Ⓓ
10 Ⓐ Ⓑ Ⓒ Ⓓ	30 Ⓐ Ⓑ Ⓒ Ⓓ	50 Ⓐ Ⓑ Ⓒ Ⓓ
11 Ⓐ Ⓑ Ⓒ Ⓓ	31 Ⓐ Ⓑ Ⓒ Ⓓ	51 Ⓐ Ⓑ Ⓒ Ⓓ
12 Ⓐ Ⓑ Ⓒ Ⓓ	32 Ⓐ Ⓑ Ⓒ Ⓓ	52 Ⓐ Ⓑ Ⓒ Ⓓ
13 Ⓐ Ⓑ Ⓒ Ⓓ	33 Ⓐ Ⓑ Ⓒ Ⓓ	53 Ⓐ Ⓑ Ⓒ Ⓓ
14 Ⓐ Ⓑ Ⓒ Ⓓ	34 Ⓐ Ⓑ Ⓒ Ⓓ	54 Ⓐ Ⓑ Ⓒ Ⓓ
15 Ⓐ Ⓑ Ⓒ Ⓓ	35 Ⓐ Ⓑ Ⓒ Ⓓ	55 Ⓐ Ⓑ Ⓒ Ⓓ
16 Ⓐ Ⓑ Ⓒ Ⓓ	36 Ⓐ Ⓑ Ⓒ Ⓓ	56 Ⓐ Ⓑ Ⓒ Ⓓ
17 Ⓐ Ⓑ Ⓒ Ⓓ	37 Ⓐ Ⓑ Ⓒ Ⓓ	57 Ⓐ Ⓑ Ⓒ Ⓓ
18 Ⓐ Ⓑ Ⓒ Ⓓ	38 Ⓐ Ⓑ Ⓒ Ⓓ	58 Ⓐ Ⓑ Ⓒ Ⓓ
19 Ⓐ Ⓑ Ⓒ Ⓓ	39 Ⓐ Ⓑ Ⓒ Ⓓ	59 Ⓐ Ⓑ Ⓒ Ⓓ
20 Ⓐ Ⓑ Ⓒ Ⓓ	40 Ⓐ Ⓑ Ⓒ Ⓓ	60 Ⓐ Ⓑ Ⓒ Ⓓ

61 Ⓐ Ⓑ Ⓒ Ⓓ	81 Ⓐ Ⓑ Ⓒ Ⓓ
62 Ⓐ Ⓑ Ⓒ Ⓓ	82 Ⓐ Ⓑ Ⓒ Ⓓ
63 Ⓐ Ⓑ Ⓒ Ⓓ	83 Ⓐ Ⓑ Ⓒ Ⓓ
64 Ⓐ Ⓑ Ⓒ Ⓓ	84 Ⓐ Ⓑ Ⓒ Ⓓ
65 Ⓐ Ⓑ Ⓒ Ⓓ	85 Ⓐ Ⓑ Ⓒ Ⓓ
66 Ⓐ Ⓑ Ⓒ Ⓓ	86 Ⓐ Ⓑ Ⓒ Ⓓ
67 Ⓐ Ⓑ Ⓒ Ⓓ	87 Ⓐ Ⓑ Ⓒ Ⓓ
68 Ⓐ Ⓑ Ⓒ Ⓓ	88 Ⓐ Ⓑ Ⓒ Ⓓ
69 Ⓐ Ⓑ Ⓒ Ⓓ	89 Ⓐ Ⓑ Ⓒ Ⓓ
70 Ⓐ Ⓑ Ⓒ Ⓓ	90 Ⓐ Ⓑ Ⓒ Ⓓ
71 Ⓐ Ⓑ Ⓒ Ⓓ	91 Ⓐ Ⓑ Ⓒ Ⓓ
72 Ⓐ Ⓑ Ⓒ Ⓓ	92 Ⓐ Ⓑ Ⓒ Ⓓ
73 Ⓐ Ⓑ Ⓒ Ⓓ	93 Ⓐ Ⓑ Ⓒ Ⓓ
74 Ⓐ Ⓑ Ⓒ Ⓓ	94 Ⓐ Ⓑ Ⓒ Ⓓ
75 Ⓐ Ⓑ Ⓒ Ⓓ	95 Ⓐ Ⓑ Ⓒ Ⓓ
76 Ⓐ Ⓑ Ⓒ Ⓓ	96 Ⓐ Ⓑ Ⓒ Ⓓ
77 Ⓐ Ⓑ Ⓒ Ⓓ	97 Ⓐ Ⓑ Ⓒ Ⓓ
78 Ⓐ Ⓑ Ⓒ Ⓓ	98 Ⓐ Ⓑ Ⓒ Ⓓ
79 Ⓐ Ⓑ Ⓒ Ⓓ	99 Ⓐ Ⓑ Ⓒ Ⓓ
80 Ⓐ Ⓑ Ⓒ Ⓓ	100 Ⓐ Ⓑ Ⓒ Ⓓ

Practice Test 2

Directions: For each of the following questions, select the choice that best answers the question.

1. During what phase of development and construction should zoning be considered?

   A. land acquisition
   B. subdivision
   C. development
   D. construction

2. Which of the following real estate professionals are usually paid a flat fee for their investment advice?

   A. appraisers
   B. brokers
   C. managers
   D. counselors

3. Which of the following is true?

   A. A CMA is an appraisal.
   B. A CMA is a marketing tool.
   C. A broker may not charge a fee for a CMA.
   D. A CMA may not use expired listings in analyzing the market.

4. Zoning and taxation as they impact the real estate market are primarily a function of the

   A. local government.
   B. state government.
   C. federal government.
   D. Real Estate Commission.

GO ON TO THE NEXT PAGE

5. The essential criteria for needing a license to perform real estate activities is

    A. performing any of the legislated list of real estate services.

    B. providing advice about real estate matters.

    C. acting as an attorney in fact.

    D. performing real estate services for a fee for another person.

6. An attorney performing real estate services

    A. never requires a real estate license.

    B. requires a real estate license if she receives compensation.

    C. always requires a real estate license.

    D. requires a real estate license when she is acting as an attorney in fact.

7. A prior conviction must be revealed on the real estate license application

    A. only if the individual pled no contest.

    B. only if court action was taken.

    C. only if the individual pled guilty.

    D. always.

8. A builder who develops and sells her own properties

    A. must have a real estate broker's license.

    B. must have at least a real estate sales associate license.

    C. is exempt from licensing requirements.

    D. must have a broker's license if she employs sales associates.

9. The owner of a timeshare who wants to sell it

    A. is exempt from licensing requirements only if the timeshare is for his own use.

    B. is exempt from licensing requirements without exception.

    C. is exempt from licensing requirements only if he owns and sells one timeshare.

    D. must have a special timeshare sales license.

10. Florida Real Estate Commission members are appointed for a term of

    A. four years.

    B. three years.

    C. two years.

    D. one year.

11. Because the Florida Real Estate Commission may grant or revoke real estate licenses and investigate license law violations, it is said to have

    A. quasi-legislative power.

    B. executive power.

    C. quasi-judicial power.

    D. administrative power.

12. The seal of the Florida Real Estate Commission, when properly used on documents, indicates that

    A. the documents may not be subject to nolo contendere.

    B. the documents are valid without further proof.

    C. the documents may only be challenged in a court of law.

    D. the documents are valid if adopted by a unanimous vote of the Florida Real Estate Commission.

Practice Test 2

GO ON TO THE NEXT PAGE

13. The longest period of time in which a real estate license can be valid is

    A. one year.
    B. 18 months.
    C. two years.
    D. It depends on your date of birth.

14. A property owner hires someone to handle all his properties except for buying and selling them. He is acting as a

    A. general agent.
    B. universal agent.
    C. special agent.
    D. managing agent.

15. Which of the following statements is true in the case of a single agency residential transaction?

    A. A broker may represent both the buyer and the seller in a fiduciary capacity.
    B. A broker may represent either the buyer or the seller in a fiduciary capacity.
    C. A customer is always represented by a broker as an agent.
    D. A seller is always represented by a broker as an agent.

16. The principal of buyer beware that exists in most common business dealings is described by the term

    A. nolo contendere.
    B. caveat vendor.
    C. caveat emptor.
    D. fiduciary representation.

17. Which of the following would least likely be considered misrepresentation or fraud in showing a property for sale?

   A. describing the property as having "beautiful landscaping," when the property has three scraggly bushes in the front of the house

   B. describing the property as being "termite-free," when the agent knows of termite problems

   C. not informing the buyer of a zoning change to commercial zoning across the street, when this fact is known to the broker

   D. not informing the buyer of construction of a waste disposal plant next to the house, which has been announced in the local newspaper but which the broker is unaware of

18. Designated sales associate status is available

   A. in all Florida real estate transactions.

   B. for nonresidential transactions only.

   C. only in cases of dual agency in residential transactions.

   D. when one broker is representing a seller and another broker is representing a buyer of the same property.

19. The primary purpose of a transition to transaction brokerage is to

   A. avoid illegal dual agency.

   B. make sure a single broker receives the full commission on a sale.

   C. reduce broker liability.

   D. make sure each party receives full agency representation.

20. Broker A pays his barber $100 for every client the barber refers to him. Which of the following statements is true about this action?

   A. This is a finder's fee and is always legal.

   B. This is a finder's fee and is legal as long as the amount is less than $200.

   C. This is a referral fee and is always legal.

   D. This is a referral fee and is illegal.

Practice Test 2

GO ON TO THE NEXT PAGE

21. Commissions and fees paid by the seller of a property

    A. must be paid to the broker directly.

    B. must be paid to the sales associate directly.

    C. may be paid to the broker or sales associate.

    D. are generally paid to the multiple listing system for division between brokers and sales associates.

22. An office located in a subdivision that is only designed to provide protection to customers and sales agents is considered a

    A. temporary shelter and must be registered.

    B. temporary shelter and need not be registered.

    C. branch office and must be registered.

    D. branch office and must be registered as a temporary shelter.

23. Commissions are

    A. always negotiable.

    B. set by the Florida Real Estate Commission.

    C. set by the local board of Realtors.

    D. set by the local multiple listing system.

24. Presuming no one was injured financially, what is the most likely punishment, if any, for advertising in such a way that a person does not know she is dealing with a real estate licensee?

    A. no penalty

    B. criminal penalty

    C. civil penalty

    D. administrative penalty

25. The minimum sentence for obtaining a real estate license by fraud is

  A. suspension.
  B. revocation.
  C. $1,000 fine.
  D. suspension or revocation and a $1,000 fine.

26. An allegation of facts and charges against a real estate licensee during the complaint process is called the

  A. formal complaint.
  B. bill of particulars.
  C. bill of charges.
  D. list of charges.

27. A minor violation of the license law would most likely be handled through a

  A. civil action.
  B. notice of noncompliance.
  C. citation.
  D. license suspension.

28. Which law deals only with race with respect to housing discrimination?

  A. Fair Housing Law of 1968
  B. Civil Rights Law of 1866
  C. Equal Credit Opportunity Act
  D. Florida Fair Housing Law

GO ON TO THE NEXT PAGE

Practice Test 2

29. A licensed real estate broker may represent someone who wants to limit the sale of his owner-occupied home to a member of a particular religious group

    A. if discriminatory advertising is not used.

    B. if permission to do so is received from the Florida Real Estate Commission.

    C. if the person owns only the one house.

    D. never.

30. Which of the following is a protected class under the Equal Credit Opportunity Act but not under the Fair Housing Law?

    A. marital status

    B. familial status

    C. national origin

    D. sex

31. Under the Interstate Land Sales Full Disclosure Act, subdivisions must be registered with HUD if they are

    A. 25 lots or more.

    B. 50 lots or more.

    C. 75 lots or more.

    D. 100 lots or more.

32. Tenants' security deposits may be

    A. placed in non-interest-bearing accounts.

    B. commingled with the landlord's operating funds if a surety bond is posted.

    C. deposited in separate interest bearing accounts.

    D. handled in any of the preceding ways.

33. Real property includes only

    A. the land.
    B. the land and structures.
    C. the land, structures, and fixtures.
    D. the land, structures, fixtures, and personal property.

34. In his will, Owner A leaves his house to his children subject to a life estate to his sister. The interest held by his children is best described as

    A. fee simple interest.
    B. remainder interest.
    C. reversionary interest.
    D. life interest.

35. Several people concurrently own a piece of property. They may not own the property as

    A. tenants in severalty.
    B. tenants in common.
    C. joint tenants.
    D. tenants in partnership.

36. Lumber is delivered to a house to build a deck. At what point, if any, does the lumber become a fixture?

    A. when it is delivered
    B. when the building permit for the deck is issued
    C. when the deck is complete
    D. None of the above—it never becomes a fixture.

GO ON TO THE NEXT PAGE

37. Which of the following will not cause a cloud on the title to real estate?

    A.   mechanic's lien

    B.   pending eminent domain action

    C.   pending action for adverse possession

    D.   pending zoning change

38. Owner A gives the county a subsurface easement across her property to build a sewer line. This is best described as an

    A.   easement appurtenant by grant.

    B.   easement in gross by grant.

    C.   easement appurtenant by condemnation.

    D.   easement in gross by condemnation.

39. When a home is sold to pay off unpaid debts, the first debt to be paid is

    A.   tax liens.

    B.   first mortgages liens.

    C.   the earliest lien filed by date.

    D.   the lien with the largest amount of money due.

40. Neighbor A built a fence 2 feet onto Owner B's property. This is best described as a(n)

    A.   easement.

    B.   encroachment.

    C.   prescriptive right.

    D.   adverse possession.

41. Owner A owns a three-story building on property that is zoned for construction of a 20-story building. Owner A does not want to sell his building but wants to make some additional money from it. Assuming his actions are in accordance with local development codes, what might he do?

A. seek a right of correlative use
B. sell his air rights
C. seek a zoning change
D. There is nothing he can do to derive additional income from his property.

42. In the government or rectangular survey system, which of the following is not true?

A. A section is 640 acres.
B. A township has 36 sections.
C. A section is a square, ½ mile on each side.
D. A township is a square, 6 miles on each side.

43. In the government survey system, when, because of natural features, a lot that is less than a quarter section was created, it was referred to as a(n)

A. odd lot.
B. survey lot.
C. substandard lot.
D. government lot.

44. Which of the following terms could be used to describe the metes and bounds method of legally describing property?

A. plat map and filed map
B. township and section
C. parcel section and lot
D. distances and directions

GO ON TO THE NEXT PAGE

45. Which of the following is not a system of legal property description?

    A. assessor's map and parcel ID
    B. metes and bounds
    C. lot and block
    D. government survey

46. An exclusive right-to-sell agreement is considered an

    A. implied unilateral contract.
    B. express unilateral contract.
    C. implied bilateral contract.
    D. express bilateral contract.

47. Owner A discusses the terms of selling his property with Buyer B. They agree on the amount of money, the type of deed, and when the closing will be. This contract for the sale of the property is

    A. valid and enforceable.
    B. void and unenforceable.
    C. valid and voidable.
    D. valid and unenforceable.

48. The major difference between a unilateral contract and a bilateral contract is that

    A. in a unilateral contract, both people must act; in a bilateral contract, only one must act.
    B. in a unilateral contract, only one party agrees to do something; in a bilateral contract, both agree to do something.
    C. in a unilateral contract, only one party must act; in a bilateral contract, both parties must act.
    D. There is no difference as long as the contract is in writing.

49. Buyer A signs an agreement with Seller B to purchase her home. Seller B changes her mind about selling, but Buyer A still wants the house. Buyer B files a suit for

   A. rescission.
   B. release.
   C. specific performance.
   D. novation.

50. A homeowner places an advertisement in the newspaper offering her home for sale and offering to compensate any broker who brings a successful buyer to the property. The homeowner is seeking to create an

   A. express bilateral option listing.
   B. express unilateral open listing.
   C. express bilateral exclusive listing.
   D. express unilateral exclusive agency listing.

51. The difference between the primary mortgage market and the secondary mortgage market is that the secondary market

   A. only lends money to member banks.
   B. buys mortgages from primary lenders.
   C. provides guarantees to lenders for borrowers who would otherwise be unqualified to buy property.
   D. subsidizes primary lenders by using creative financing.

52. What is the loan-to-value ratio above which a borrower will typically have to purchase private mortgage insurance?

   A. 100%
   B. 95%
   C. 90%
   D. 80%

GO ON TO THE NEXT PAGE

53. A conforming loan is defined as one

    A. for an amount that meets Federal National Mortgage Association (FNMA) standards.

    B. for a house in a neighborhood of conforming properties.

    C. that is protected by private mortgage insurance (PMI).

    D. that is fully amortized.

54. An acceleration clause in a mortgage loan

    A. allows the borrower to make advance payments on principal.

    B. allows the borrower to renegotiate the interest rate.

    C. allows the lender to sell the loan to another lender.

    D. allows the lender to declare the entire loan amount due immediately.

55. Among other activities, which of the following does the Federal Reserve System do to control the supply of money available for loans?

    A. print money

    B. control the rate at which the secondary market may purchase loans

    C. set the discount rate

    D. set the inflation rate

56. In a loan situation, what does a mortgage do?

    A. It provides the lender with a promise to pay.

    B. It sets the terms of the loan.

    C. It turns over title to the property until the loan is paid off.

    D. It acts as the security instrument for the loan.

57. A deed in lieu of foreclosure

    A. will avoid a foreclosure sale.

    B. is executed after the foreclosure sale.

    C. benefits the beneficiary if the property is worth less than the amount owed on the mortgage.

    D. is the same as a reconveyance deed.

58. Which of the following is true of VA loans?

    A. The buyer cannot pay more than the appraised value.

    B. The VA requires a down payment.

    C. The VA guarantee can be for more than the appraised value.

    D. The lender can require a down payment.

59. The secondary mortgage market includes all of the following except

    A. FNMA.

    B. FDIC.

    C. GNMA.

    D. FHLMC.

60. A double entry item on the buyer's and seller's closing statements

    A. is a debit to both parties.

    B. is a credit to both parties.

    C. is a credit to one party and a debit to the other party.

    D. includes attorney's fees.

GO ON TO THE NEXT PAGE

Practice Test 2

61. Unpaid property taxes appear on a closing statement as a

    A. credit to the buyer and the seller.
    B. debit to the buyer and the seller.
    C. credit to the buyer and a debit to the seller.
    D. credit to the seller and a debit to the buyer.

62. Taxes are paid in arrears on a property. How will the prorated amount appear on the closing statements?

    A. credit to buyer; debit to seller
    B. debit to buyer; credit to seller
    C. credit to seller; no entry for buyer
    D. debit to seller; no entry for buyer

63. The state intangible tax applies to the recording of

    A. deeds.
    B. mortgages.
    C. notes.
    D. easements.

64. According to federal regulations, a licensed or certified appraiser is required for all federally related transaction appraisals for properties valued above

    A. $50,000.
    B. $100,000.
    C. $200,000.
    D. $250,000.

65. In the cost approach to valuation, the cost to create an exact duplicate of the building is called its

  A. replacement cost.
  B. depreciated cost.
  C. rebuilding cost.
  D. reproduction cost.

66. In the sales comparison approach, adjustments are made to

  A. the subject to make it like the comparable.
  B. the comparable to make it like the subject.
  C. one comparable to make it like another comparable.
  D. both the subject and the comparable.

67. In the cost approach, accrued depreciation is

  A. added to the reproduction or replacement cost.
  B. deducted from the replacement or reproduction cost.
  C. only based on physical deterioration.
  D. only calculated if the structure is more than ten years old.

68. "The value of a property is determined by the cost to purchase a property of similar usefulness" is a good definition of the principle of

  A. progression.
  B. change.
  C. highest and best use.
  D. substitution.

GO ON TO THE NEXT PAGE

69. A person who wants to act as his own general contractor to build a house would consult what official document to determine the amount of insulation mandated by law?

    A.   zoning ordinance

    B.   home warranty

    C.   plans and specifications

    D.   building code

70. Which type of window can provide the largest opening for ventilation relative to the amount of glass?

    A.   casement

    B.   sliding

    C.   double hung

    D.   fixed

71. The term *built-up roof* is commonly associated with what type of roof?

    A.   flat

    B.   gambrel

    C.   mansard

    D.   gable

72. Wider open spaces with fewer interior supporting columns is a feature of what type of house framing?

    A.   balloon

    B.   platform

    C.   post and beam

    D.   saltbox

73. Inflation is a primary consideration analyzing what type of risk in an investment?

    A. business risk

    B. financial risk

    C. purchasing power risk

    D. interest rate risk

74. The goal of leverage in a real estate investment is to

    A. maximize equity

    B. make the investment more liquid

    C. increase the return on equity

    D. decrease cash flow

75. Depreciable assets of a furniture store business could include all but which of the following?

    A. furniture stock

    B. delivery trucks

    C. land used for truck parking

    D. loading equipment

76. Everything a business owns (like land or equipment) or is entitled to (like money owed to the business) is called its

    A. equity

    B. capital

    C. liabilities

    D. assets

GO ON TO THE NEXT PAGE

77. In an investment interest rate, risk will affect

    A. gross income.

    B. net income.

    C. cash flow.

    D. purchasing power.

78. Florida statutes require that, for tax purposes, all properties be assessed at

    A. just value.

    B. real value.

    C. market value.

    D. appraised value.

79. What law was designed to protect Florida's agricultural land from excessive taxation?

    A. Save Our Home Amendment

    B. Homestead Act

    C. Green Belt Law

    D. Farm Exemption Act

80. The town decides to put in sidewalks in your neighborhood and expects all the residents in the neighborhood to pay for this improvement. This would normally be paid through

    A. sales tax.

    B. ad valorem tax.

    C. improvement district tax.

    D. special assessment tax.

81. What is the earliest time after the purchase of a tax certificate in which the holder can force a sale of the property?

   A.   one year
   B.   two years
   C.   three years
   D.   seven years

82. Which of the following is true regarding the purchase of property in the United States from a foreign owner?

   A.   The buyer must pay all cash.
   B.   The seller must be a resident alien.
   C.   The buyer must withhold a portion of the sale price.
   D.   The seller must reside in the country for at least 90 days prior to the sale.

83. An excess supply of housing units generally creates a(n)

   A.   balanced market.
   B.   buyer's market.
   C.   seller's market.
   D.   equilibrium market.

84. In general, what effect will a rise in mortgage interest rates have on real estate prices?

   A.   Prices will rise.
   B.   Prices will go down.
   C.   Housing prices will be unaffected, but commercial property prices will rise.
   D.   Real estate prices will be unaffected.

GO ON TO THE NEXT PAGE

Practice Test 2

85. The fact that each piece of property is unique is best described by the term

   A. homogeneous.
   B. heterogeneous.
   C. indestructible.
   D. immobile.

86. A government document addressing the future physical development, transportation, housing, and other issues is called the

   A. zoning ordinance.
   B. comprehensive or master plan.
   C. building code.
   D. subdivision map law.

87. Funeral homes are sometimes permitted in some residential areas, as long as certain specific requirements are met. Someone wanting to build a funeral home in such a residential area will most likely have to apply for a(n)

   A. conditional use permit.
   B. use variance.
   C. area variance.
   D. special exception.

88. Which of the following types of projects would least likely be required to submit an environmental impact statement?

   A. building permit for a single-family house
   B. development plan for a large shopping center
   C. proposed development of regional impact
   D. approval of a tentative subdivision plan

89. When a person's land is rezoned to a use that reduces the value of the land by 25%, the owner

    A. is entitled to proportional compensation.

    B. is entitled to no compensation.

    C. has a claim under eminent domain law.

    D. can claim compensatory damages.

90. A subdivider plans on turning over the streets in a subdivision to the local town. This is most correctly called a

    A. grant.

    B. conveyance.

    C. devise.

    D. dedication.

91. Owner A is selling the northwest quarter of a section of land he owns. How much land is he selling?

    A. 40 acres

    B. 160 acres

    C. 320 acres

    D. 640 acres

92. Using the gross rent multiplier method, what is the value of a residential property improved with a four-unit building where each unit rents for $750 per month and the typical multiplier is 157?

    A. $471,000

    B. $391,000

    C. $241,300

    D. $117,000

GO ON TO THE NEXT PAGE

Practice Test 2

93. A subject property has four bedrooms. The comparable property has three bedrooms and recently sold for $225,000. The value of a bedroom is estimated to be $30,000. In all other respects, the properties are the same. What is the indicated value of the subject property?

    A. $195,000

    B. $225,000

    C. $255,000

    D. Not enough information is provided.

94. If the reproduction cost of a house is $300,000 with an economic life of 50 years, how much does the house depreciate each year using the straight-line method of calculating depreciation?

    A. $10,000

    B. $6,000

    C. $5,000

    D. $2,000

95. Buyer A is purchasing a home for $375,000 and is getting a mortgage loan at a loan-to-value ratio of 80%. The lender is charging 2 points to secure a lower interest rate. How much will the borrower have to pay in points?

    A. $3,750

    B. $6,000

    C. $7,500

    D. $75,000

96. What is the first month's interest on an amortized 30-year loan for $250,000 at 7% interest?

    A. $17,500

    B. $1,750

    C. $1,458

    D. $583

97. A seller pays the yearly taxes of $1,825 in arrears on December 31. He closes on the sale of the house on December 22. Who owes what to whom?

A. The buyer owes the seller $1,725.
B. The seller owes the buyer $1,725.
C. The buyer owes the seller $50.
D. The seller owes the buyer $50.

98. A borrower obtains a fully amortized mortgage loan for $165,000 at an interest rate of 6.5% for 30 years. The monthly payments are $1,044.45. What is the balance of the principal after the first month's payment?

A. $164,849.30
B. $163,955.55
C. $107,250
D. $893.75

99. PMI will no longer be necessary on a 100% LTV ratio loan of $178,000 when the LTV reaches 75%. The property, having appreciated in value, is now worth $210,000. How much of the principal of the loan will have to be paid off before the PMI can be dropped?

A. None—PMI can be dropped immediately.
B. $10,000
C. $17,000
D. $20,500

100. Payment of 3 points on a note whose rate is 6% will increase the yield to the lender to

A. 6⅛%
B. 6¼%
C. 6⅜%
D. 6½%

Answer Key for Practice Test 2

1. A		**31.** D
2. D		**32.** D
3. B		**33.** C
4. A		**34.** B
5. D		**35.** A
6. B		**36.** C
7. D		**37.** D
8. C		**38.** B
9. A		**39.** A
10. A		**40.** B
11. C		**41.** B
12. B		**42.** C
13. C		**43.** D.
14. A		**44.** D
15. B		**45.** A
16. C		**46.** D
17. A		**47.** B
18. B		**48.** C
19. A		**49.** C
20. D		**50.** B
21. A		**51.** B
22. B		**52.** D
23. A		**53.** A
24. D		**54.** D
25. D		**55.** C
26. A		**56.** D
27. B		**57.** A
28. B		**58.** D
29. D		**59.** B
30. A		**60.** C

61.	C	**81.**	B
62.	A	**82.**	C
63.	B	**83.**	B
64.	D	**84.**	B
65.	D	**85.**	B
66.	B	**86.**	B
67.	B	**87.**	D
68.	D	**88.**	A
69.	D	**89.**	B
70.	A	**90.**	D
71.	A	**91.**	B
72.	C	**92.**	A
73.	C	**93.**	C
74.	C	**94.**	B
75.	C	**95.**	B
76.	D	**96.**	C
77.	C	**97.**	C
78.	A	**98.**	A
79.	C	**99.**	D
80.	D	**100.**	C

Answers and Explanations for Practice Test 2

1. **A.** Because zoning will dictate what can be built, as well as density of development, it should be considered when land is acquired.

2. **D.** Though appraisers are usually paid a flat fee and managers might be paid a flat fee, counselors are the only ones who are hired specifically to give investment advice.

3. **B.** This is definitional and statutory.

4. **A.** This is statutory.

5. **D.** A person can perform any of the services for himself and, theoretically, could help a friend or family member with real estate activities for his property with no fee expectation. How a person gets paid (commission or fee based) doesn't change the licensing requirements. But any of the legislated list of services performed for a fee for another person requires licensing.

6. **B.** This is statutory. Attorneys in fact (usually people acting under a power of attorney to sign documents) are exempt.

7. **D.** All prior convictions must be reported.

8. **C.** Owner-developers are exempt from licensing requirements and may employ licensed sales associates.

9. **A.** This is a statutory exemption.

10. **A.** They may also only serve a maximum of two consecutive terms.

11. **C.** Judicial power is the power associated with administering and dealing with violations of the law.

12. **B.** This is statutory.

13. **C.** This is statutory because expiration dates are fixed on March 31 and September 30.

14. **A.** Property managers are considered general agents because they handle a range of activities.

15. **B.** This is statutory. Choice A would be dual agency, which is prohibited by Florida law.

16. **C.** This is definitional.

17. **A.** Because the landscaping would be readily visible, it is the least likely choice to be considered misrepresentation. The broker knew of, or should have known of, the other situations.

18. **B.** This is statutory. A designated sales associate can be used when two sales associates work for the same broker in a transaction on the same piece of nonresidential property.

19. **A.** Dual agency is illegal, which is the primary purpose of creating the transition option to a transaction broker relationship. The result is reduced liability, because the broker won't be breaking the law and it will allow the broker to receive the full commission. But neither of these is the primary purpose of the law allowing this transition. Agency representation is essentially reduced to nothing in this option.

20. **D.** If you read this question carefully, choices A and C are essentially the same thing.

21. **A.** Only a broker may receive a fee or commission. The sales associate then receives her share from the broker.

22. **B.** This is statutory. If the office is set up specifically as an office (office supplies and equipment, sales associates assigned there), it becomes a branch office and must be registered.

23. **A.** Commissions are always negotiable between broker and client.

24. **D.** An administrative penalty by means of a citation would be the most likely way this type of offense would be dealt with.

25. **D.** This is statutory.

26. **A.** This is definitional within the complaint process.

27. B. The notice of noncompliance gives the violator 15 days to comply.

28. B. The 1866 Civil Rights Act only deals with racial discrimination in housing.

29. D. A real estate licensee is held to a higher standard and may not represent someone even if the exemption is available to the seller.

30. A. The other protected classes not covered in the Federal Fair Housing Act are age and source of income.

31. D. This is statutory.

32. D. This is part of the Florida Residential Landlord and Tenant Act.

33. C. Real property does not include personal property.

34. B. The children have only a partial interest in the property. The possessory interest remains. Therefore, they have a remainder interest.

35. A. Tenancy in severalty is ownership by only one person. All the other forms of ownership are for two or more people.

36. C. The lumber is personal property until the deck is built and becomes a part of the real estate.

37. D. Choices A, B, and C limit, or may limit, the ownership of the property. Although zoning may affect profitability or value, it does not affect title to a property.

38. B. You have to examine both parts of each answer as it relates to the question. Because this easement does not benefit an adjacent landowner, it is not an easement appurtenant. This eliminates choices A and C. Owner A gave the easement to the county; the county did not take the easement against her will. This eliminates eminent domain (Choice D).

39. A. This is known as the priority of liens and, in general, tax liens are always first regardless of date filed.

40. B. This encroachment may eventually become an adverse possession or prescriptive easement situation, but until it does, it is an encroachment.

41. B. There are likely a number of things he can do, including tearing down the building and rebuilding; this was not a choice, but it does eliminate Choice D. Choice A relates to water rights, and he already has zoning, which would allow him to build a bigger building.

42. C. A section is a mile long on each side.

43. D. These lots were numbered and called government lots.

44. D. This is definitional. The other terms refer to other systems of description.

45. A. The assessor's map and parcel ID is used for tax purposes not legal description.

46. D. The agent's promise to market the property and the seller's promise to compensate the agent are generally expressed in writing.

47. B. Because all real estate sales contracts must be in writing, the contract is both void and unenforceable.

48. C. Don't be confused by Choice B. In both types of contracts, both parties agree to do something. The difference is stated in Choice C.

49. C. The suit for specific performance is the method for forcing a party to a contract to fulfill the terms of the contract.

50. B. Because the homeowner has expressed her terms and will pay only if a broker produces a buyer, Choice B is correct. The other answers are essentially random combinations of the terms involved in contracts and listings.

51. B. The role of the secondary market is to keep mortgage money in circulation by buying mortgage loans from primary lenders.

52. D. The way this question is worded, you could argue that all the answers are correct, but question writers will often ask questions like this meaning the lowest amount above which private mortgage insurance must be purchased.

53. A. A conforming loan meets FNMA underwriting standards and limits on the loan amount.

54. D. An acceleration clause allows the lender to declare the full loan due immediately under certain circumstances such as the buyer's defaulting on the loan.

55. C. The Federal Reserve System has no control over the other choices.

56. D. A mortgage is a security instrument for a real estate loan but does not turn over title.

57. A. A deed in lieu of foreclosure transfers the property to the lender voluntarily without a foreclosure process.

58. D. The opposite is true of each of the incorrect answers.

59. B. The Federal Deposit Insurance Corporation (FDIC) insures deposits. It is not part of the secondary mortgage market.

60. C. The concept of double entry refers to the fact that the item will be paid by one party and owed to the other party.

61. C. Look carefully at the wording of this question. If the property taxes are unpaid it means the seller owes them, so the seller gets a debit and the buyer gets a credit.

62. A. The prorated amount will be have to be paid by the seller (debit) and credited to the buyer (credit). What will not appear on the buyer's closing statement is the amount of tax he will have to pay in the future.

63. B. This is statutory. There is also a documentary stamp tax that is charged to record the note or promise to pay. Remember the mortgage is not the promise to pay but establishes the lien on the property.

64. D. The cutoff point for residential properties in federally related transactions is $250,000.

65. D. Replacement cost is for a duplicate building using updated materials. *Rebuilding cost* is not a term used in the cost approach. The depreciated cost comes after depreciation is deducted from either the reproduction or replacement cost.

66. B. The sales comparison method calls for differences between the comparable properties and the subject property to be accounted for by making adjustments to each comparable property individually to render it as much like the subject property as possible.

67. B. Total depreciation from all sources, also known as *accrued depreciation,* is calculated on any building where it is present regardless of age and is then deducted from either the reproduction cost or replacement cost.

68. D. The principle of substitution says that the maximum value of a property will be related to the cost of obtaining a property of similar usefulness.

69. D. Plans and specifications should reflect the legal requirements, but the ultimate source of the required insulations standards is the building code.

70. A. All the other windows open only partially or not at all (fixed). The casement window completely swings out opening 100% of the glass area.

71. A. This is definitional—the flat roof is usually constructed in layers.

72. C. Choice D is actually an architectural style not a type of framing.

73. C. This is definitional. Purchasing power—how much a dollar will buy—is affected negatively by rising inflation.

74. C. When a property is first purchased, equity is initially the amount of money invested by the investor. Leverage—the use of borrowed funds—allows the investor to use less of her own money. Since the dollar amount of return from the property remains the same regardless of how much of her own cash the investor puts into the investment, the less cash she puts in, the higher the percentage of return.

75. C. Land never depreciates. Equipment and furniture generally depreciate in value.

76. D. This is definitional.

77. C. Expenses except debt service (mortgage payments) are subtracted from gross income to arrive at net income. So changing mortgage rates would not affect net income. Debt service is subtracted from net income to arrive at cash flow, making Choice C correct.

78. A. This is statutory.

79. C. Choice D is made up. The Green Belt Law provides for somewhat favorable tax treatment of agricultural properties.

80. D. This is definitional.

81. B. This is statutory.

82. C. As a protection from avoiding tax payments, when buying property from a foreign seller, a buyer must withhold 10% of the purchase price and forward it to the federal government.

83. B. Because buyers have more choices when there is excess supply, this condition is called a *buyer's market.*

84. B. As interest rates rise, a person's income does not go as far in purchasing power with respect to mortgage money.

85. B. Another term for heterogeneous is *nonhomogenous.*

86. B. This is definitional. The wrong answer choices cover more-specific issues than the general plan.

87. D. Special exceptions (sometimes referred to as *special exception uses* or *permits*) are for uses that may be somewhat compatible with a particular zoning district but require additional review and approval.

88. A. Individual building permits would normally be considered to have minimal environmental impact and among the answer choices would have the least environmental impact.

89. B. Normally, a person is entitled to compensation only when the all reasonable use of the property has been denied.

90. D. Although all the terms imply some form of transfer of ownership of property, the correct term for this type of conveyance in connection with a subdivision is *dedication.*

91. B. You need to remember that a section contains 640 acres. One-quarter of a section is 0.25×640, or 160 acres.

92. A. First, you multiply the $750 rental by 4 to account for the four units in the building: $750 \times 4 = \$3,000$ gross monthly rent. The formula you want to use is

Monthly Rental Income $\times$ Gross Rent Multiplier = Value

$3,000 \times 157 = \$471,000$.

93. C. The value of the bedroom is added to the sales price of the comparable in order to make the comparable (three bedrooms) like the subject (four bedrooms): $225,000 + \$30,000 = \$255,000$.

94. B. Straight-line depreciation assumes that the entire cost of the house depreciates at an equal rate per year over the assumed lifetime (economic life) of the house.

Reproduction or Replacement Cost of House $\div$ Economic Life of House = Annual Depreciation

$300,000 \div 50$ years $= \$6,000$ per year depreciation

95. B. A point is 1% of the loan amount.

$375,000 (Purchase Price) $\times$ 0.80 (Loan-to-Value Ratio) = \$300,000 (Amount of Mortgage)

$300,000 (Amount of Mortgage) $\times$ 0.02 (Number of Points) = \$6,000 (Amount Paid in Points)

Remember that to multiply percentages you have to convert to a decimal, so 80% = 0.80 and 2% = 0.02.

96. **C.** The 30-year term is irrelevant.

$250,000 × 0.07 = $17,500 (First Year's Interest)

$17,500 ÷ 12 months = $1,458 (rounded)

97. **C.** The seller has paid the taxes for the current tax period, which is the entire previous year. However, the seller will not own the house for the entire tax period. The buyer will own the house from December 22. The buyer will owe the seller for a portion of the taxes already paid. The seller gets a credit and the buyer is charged with a debit. Remember that, unless otherwise stated in the problem, you have to assume that the buyer will pay for the day of closing.

$1,825 ÷ 365 days = $35 per day

$5 per day × 10 days = $50 taxes owed by the buyer to the seller.

98. **A.** *Remember:* The monthly payment on an amortized loan includes principal and interest.

$165,000 (Loan Amount) × 0.065 (Annual Interest Rate) = $10,725 (First Year's Interest)

$10,725 (First Year's Interest) ÷ 12 months = $893.75 (First Month's Interest Payoff)

$1,044.45 (First Month's Principal and Interest Payment) – $893.75 (First Month's Interest Payoff) = $150.70 (Principal Payoff)

$165,000 (Loan Amount) – $150.70 (First Month's Principal Payoff) = $164,849.30 balance

99. **D.** PMI can be dropped when the loan amount reaches 75% of the value of the property. If the property is now worth $210,000, then:

$210,000 × 0.75 = $157,500 (the amount to which the loan must be reduced)

$178,000 (original loan amount) – $157,500 = $20,500 (the amount that must be paid off)

100. **C.** Each point increases the yield to a lender by approximately ⅛%.

Answer Sheet for Practice Test 3

CUT HERE

1 Ⓐ Ⓑ Ⓒ Ⓓ	21 Ⓐ Ⓑ Ⓒ Ⓓ	41 Ⓐ Ⓑ Ⓒ Ⓓ
2 Ⓐ Ⓑ Ⓒ Ⓓ	22 Ⓐ Ⓑ Ⓒ Ⓓ	42 Ⓐ Ⓑ Ⓒ Ⓓ
3 Ⓐ Ⓑ Ⓒ Ⓓ	23 Ⓐ Ⓑ Ⓒ Ⓓ	43 Ⓐ Ⓑ Ⓒ Ⓓ
4 Ⓐ Ⓑ Ⓒ Ⓓ	24 Ⓐ Ⓑ Ⓒ Ⓓ	44 Ⓐ Ⓑ Ⓒ Ⓓ
5 Ⓐ Ⓑ Ⓒ Ⓓ	25 Ⓐ Ⓑ Ⓒ Ⓓ	45 Ⓐ Ⓑ Ⓒ Ⓓ
6 Ⓐ Ⓑ Ⓒ Ⓓ	26 Ⓐ Ⓑ Ⓒ Ⓓ	46 Ⓐ Ⓑ Ⓒ Ⓓ
7 Ⓐ Ⓑ Ⓒ Ⓓ	27 Ⓐ Ⓑ Ⓒ Ⓓ	47 Ⓐ Ⓑ Ⓒ Ⓓ
8 Ⓐ Ⓑ Ⓒ Ⓓ	28 Ⓐ Ⓑ Ⓒ Ⓓ	48 Ⓐ Ⓑ Ⓒ Ⓓ
9 Ⓐ Ⓑ Ⓒ Ⓓ	29 Ⓐ Ⓑ Ⓒ Ⓓ	49 Ⓐ Ⓑ Ⓒ Ⓓ
10 Ⓐ Ⓑ Ⓒ Ⓓ	30 Ⓐ Ⓑ Ⓒ Ⓓ	50 Ⓐ Ⓑ Ⓒ Ⓓ
11 Ⓐ Ⓑ Ⓒ Ⓓ	31 Ⓐ Ⓑ Ⓒ Ⓓ	51 Ⓐ Ⓑ Ⓒ Ⓓ
12 Ⓐ Ⓑ Ⓒ Ⓓ	32 Ⓐ Ⓑ Ⓒ Ⓓ	52 Ⓐ Ⓑ Ⓒ Ⓓ
13 Ⓐ Ⓑ Ⓒ Ⓓ	33 Ⓐ Ⓑ Ⓒ Ⓓ	53 Ⓐ Ⓑ Ⓒ Ⓓ
14 Ⓐ Ⓑ Ⓒ Ⓓ	34 Ⓐ Ⓑ Ⓒ Ⓓ	54 Ⓐ Ⓑ Ⓒ Ⓓ
15 Ⓐ Ⓑ Ⓒ Ⓓ	35 Ⓐ Ⓑ Ⓒ Ⓓ	55 Ⓐ Ⓑ Ⓒ Ⓓ
16 Ⓐ Ⓑ Ⓒ Ⓓ	36 Ⓐ Ⓑ Ⓒ Ⓓ	56 Ⓐ Ⓑ Ⓒ Ⓓ
17 Ⓐ Ⓑ Ⓒ Ⓓ	37 Ⓐ Ⓑ Ⓒ Ⓓ	57 Ⓐ Ⓑ Ⓒ Ⓓ
18 Ⓐ Ⓑ Ⓒ Ⓓ	38 Ⓐ Ⓑ Ⓒ Ⓓ	58 Ⓐ Ⓑ Ⓒ Ⓓ
19 Ⓐ Ⓑ Ⓒ Ⓓ	39 Ⓐ Ⓑ Ⓒ Ⓓ	59 Ⓐ Ⓑ Ⓒ Ⓓ
20 Ⓐ Ⓑ Ⓒ Ⓓ	40 Ⓐ Ⓑ Ⓒ Ⓓ	60 Ⓐ Ⓑ Ⓒ Ⓓ

61 Ⓐ Ⓑ Ⓒ Ⓓ	81 Ⓐ Ⓑ Ⓒ Ⓓ
62 Ⓐ Ⓑ Ⓒ Ⓓ	82 Ⓐ Ⓑ Ⓒ Ⓓ
63 Ⓐ Ⓑ Ⓒ Ⓓ	83 Ⓐ Ⓑ Ⓒ Ⓓ
64 Ⓐ Ⓑ Ⓒ Ⓓ	84 Ⓐ Ⓑ Ⓒ Ⓓ
65 Ⓐ Ⓑ Ⓒ Ⓓ	85 Ⓐ Ⓑ Ⓒ Ⓓ
66 Ⓐ Ⓑ Ⓒ Ⓓ	86 Ⓐ Ⓑ Ⓒ Ⓓ
67 Ⓐ Ⓑ Ⓒ Ⓓ	87 Ⓐ Ⓑ Ⓒ Ⓓ
68 Ⓐ Ⓑ Ⓒ Ⓓ	88 Ⓐ Ⓑ Ⓒ Ⓓ
69 Ⓐ Ⓑ Ⓒ Ⓓ	89 Ⓐ Ⓑ Ⓒ Ⓓ
70 Ⓐ Ⓑ Ⓒ Ⓓ	90 Ⓐ Ⓑ Ⓒ Ⓓ
71 Ⓐ Ⓑ Ⓒ Ⓓ	91 Ⓐ Ⓑ Ⓒ Ⓓ
72 Ⓐ Ⓑ Ⓒ Ⓓ	92 Ⓐ Ⓑ Ⓒ Ⓓ
73 Ⓐ Ⓑ Ⓒ Ⓓ	93 Ⓐ Ⓑ Ⓒ Ⓓ
74 Ⓐ Ⓑ Ⓒ Ⓓ	94 Ⓐ Ⓑ Ⓒ Ⓓ
75 Ⓐ Ⓑ Ⓒ Ⓓ	95 Ⓐ Ⓑ Ⓒ Ⓓ
76 Ⓐ Ⓑ Ⓒ Ⓓ	96 Ⓐ Ⓑ Ⓒ Ⓓ
77 Ⓐ Ⓑ Ⓒ Ⓓ	97 Ⓐ Ⓑ Ⓒ Ⓓ
78 Ⓐ Ⓑ Ⓒ Ⓓ	98 Ⓐ Ⓑ Ⓒ Ⓓ
79 Ⓐ Ⓑ Ⓒ Ⓓ	99 Ⓐ Ⓑ Ⓒ Ⓓ
80 Ⓐ Ⓑ Ⓒ Ⓓ	100 Ⓐ Ⓑ Ⓒ Ⓓ

CUT HERE

Practice Test 3

Directions: For each of the following questions, select the choice that best answers the question.

1. Which of the following is true?

   A. All brokers are Realtors.
   B. Some brokers and sales associates are Realtors.
   C. Membership in the National Association of Realtors is mandated by state law.
   D. You may use the term *Realtor* after you obtain a broker's or sales associate's license.

2. A real estate broker may arrange financing for a home sale and be paid for that service if

   A. the sale was her listing.
   B. she represented the buyer.
   C. she holds a mortgage broker's license.
   D. the mortgage amount was less than $250,000.

3. A property manager's function is to

   A. protect the owner's investment.
   B. maximize income.
   C. neither A nor B
   D. both A and B

4. The document submitted for approval to the local planning agency for approval of a subdivision is called the

   A. recorded map.
   B. filed map.
   C. planning map.
   D. subdivision plat map.

GO ON TO THE NEXT PAGE

5. Whether an employee of a company that sells or exchanges properties needs a real estate license will depend on

   A. the specific services provided.
   B. the form of compensation.
   C. neither A nor B, because they would be exempt
   D. both A and B

6. The exemption for licensing for mobile home rentals applies to

   A. all mobile home transactions.
   B. mobile home rentals in a mobile home park.
   C. mobile home rentals on individually owned lots.
   D. None of the above—there is no exemption.

7. Mutual recognition agreements

   A. automatically grant licensure to license holders from other states.
   B. require passing the broker's or sales associate's license exams.
   C. apply to new residents only.
   D. require passing a Florida real estate law exam.

8. The circumstance in which a real estate purchaser is on his own and not protected by law may be characterized by the phrase

   A. caveat vendor.
   B. caveat emptor.
   C. nolo contendere.
   D. e pluribus unum.

9. Which of the following does not have direct involvement in the regulation of real estate activities in Florida?

   A. Real Estate Commission
   B. Department of Consumer Affairs
   C. Division of Real Estate
   D. Department of Business and Professional Regulation

10. Florida Real Estate Commission members are

   A. elected.
   B. appointed by the state senate.
   C. appointed by the State Association of Realtors.
   D. appointed by the governor.

11. Continuing education and post licensing education must be completed

   A. before license renewal.
   B. within three months of license renewal.
   C. within six months of license renewal.
   D. within a year of license renewal.

12. Real estate licenses expire

   A. two years after the day they are issued.
   B. on March 31 and September 30.
   C. on the license holder's birthday.
   D. on June 30.

GO ON TO THE NEXT PAGE

13. Which of the following is not involved in the administration of Florida real estate licensing?

   A. Department of Business and Professional Regulation
   B. Division of Real Estate
   C. Florida Real Estate Commission
   D. Educational Testing Service

14. According to Florida real estate law, a person who chooses limited representation under the transaction broker relationship is a(n)

   A. principal.
   B. client.
   C. agent.
   D. customer.

15. A transaction broker

   A. represents buyer and seller as a fiduciary in the same transaction.
   B. represents neither buyer nor seller as a fiduciary in the same transaction.
   C. has a fiduciary relationship with the seller but a customer relationship with the buyer.
   D. is a dual agent.

16. In a single agent relationship, a sales associate working for a broker will

   A. be a fiduciary of the principal.
   B. be a subagent of the broker.
   C. owe obedience to both the broker and the principal.
   D. all of the above

17. A broker acting on behalf of a seller as a single agent receives two offers on a property. One offer is all cash at less than the asking price. The other offer is a for full asking price but involves the buyer obtaining a VA loan. What should the broker do with the offers?

   A. wait until the VA loan is approved before presenting the offer to the seller

   B. present only the full price offer to the seller because it is the higher price offer

   C. present only the cash offer to the seller because it will mean a fast closing

   D. present both offers to the seller as soon as possible

18. Which of the following relationships does not require agency disclosure when working with a residential customer or client?

   A. transactional brokerage

   B. single agent representation

   C. no brokerage representation

   D. none of the above

19. Which of the following is true about a no-brokerage relationship?

   A. A broker can enter into a listing agreement with a seller.

   B. A broker cannot work with a buyer because buyers must be represented.

   C. A broker can work with a buyer but must be paid by the buyer.

   D. A broker must provide full fiduciary duties to whomever she works with even if no agency relationship exists.

20. Advance listing fees

   A. may be withdrawn to cover broker office expenses.

   B. may be used for advertising the property after advising the seller.

   C. may be kept in the same account as regular brokerage operating funds.

   D. are prohibited in Florida.

GO ON TO THE NEXT PAGE

21. Exaggerating characteristics of the property that can easily be verified is a good definition of

    A. fraudulent advertising.
    B. false promises.
    C. puffing.
    D. material fact disclosure.

22. The primary requirement for a person to run a sole proprietorship real estate brokerage is

    A. a board of directors.
    B. a trade name.
    C. liability insurance.
    D. a valid broker's license.

23. The unauthorized use of another person's personal property—such as client's funds entrusted to the broker—is called

    A. commingling.
    B. conversion.
    C. escrow.
    D. transition.

24. Who or what reviews the charges in the case of a complaint about a law violation by a real estate licensee to determine if there is sufficient cause to proceed to a hearing?

    A. Florida Real Estate Commission
    B. Department of Business and Professional Regulation
    C. Probable Cause Panel (consisting of two members of the FREC)
    D. B or C but not A

25. A formal hearing on a violation of law involving a real estate licensee is

   A. held by the Florida Real Estate Commission if the licensee denies the charges.
   B. held in a civil court if the licensee denies the charges.
   C. held before an administrative law judge if the licensee denies the charges.
   D. never held. All hearings are informal.

26. The final order in the case of a complaint brought against a real estate licensee is issued by

   A. an administrative law judge.
   B. the Florida Real Estate Commission with Probable Cause Panel members excluded.
   C. the Probable Cause Panel.
   D. the Department of Business and Professional Regulation.

27. Practicing real estate activities for compensation without a license may result in fines up to

   A. $1,000.
   B. $2,500.
   C. $4,000.
   D. $5,000.

28. The court case that affirmed the 1866 Civil Rights Act and the fact that it had no exceptions with respect to racial discrimination in housing was

   A. *United States v. Foley.*
   B. *Brown v. Board of Education.*
   C. *Jones v. Mayer.*
   D. *Johnson v. Davis.*

GO ON TO THE NEXT PAGE

29. "I think you'll be happier in this neighborhood than that one because this one is mostly people like you" might be construed as

   A. redlining.
   B. blockbusting.
   C. steering.
   D. testing.

30. The Americans with Disabilities Act requires that handicapped accommodations be constructed in

   A. all multifamily buildings.
   B. multifamily buildings built since the act was passed.
   C. all multifamily buildings of more than ten units.
   D. only commercial buildings.

31. A contract to buy a lot covered by the Interstate Land Sales Full Disclosure Act may be revoked up to

   A. three days after signing.
   B. five days after signing.
   C. seven days after signing.
   D. three days after closing.

32. How long must a landlord allow a tenant to pay unpaid rent after notifying the tenant before she may begin eviction proceedings?

   A. one day
   B. three days
   C. five days
   D. seven days

33. The type of ownership that provides the most complete bundle of rights is

    A.   fee simple qualified.

    B.   fee simple absolute.

    C.   fee simple defeasible.

    D.   fee simple freehold.

34. Which of the following best describes the interests of the holder of a life estate?

    A.   possession

    B.   possession and use

    C.   possession, use, and ownership

    D.   possession, use, and ownership—but only as long as they live

35. The requirement that multiple owners take title to property at the same time is a characteristic of

    A.   ownership in severalty.

    B.   joint tenancy.

    C.   tenancy in common.

    D.   all forms of concurrent ownership.

36. Which of the following is not true about the rights of a tenant in a lease situation?

    A.   The tenant has a less than freehold estate.

    B.   The tenant has a leasehold interest.

    C.   The interest that the tenant has is considered personal property.

    D.   The tenant has a fee simple defeasible interest.

GO ON TO THE NEXT PAGE

37. The authority to adopt zoning ordinances is derived from the

  A. police power.
  B. eminent domain law.
  C. law of escheat.
  D. subdivision laws.

38. A testator who dies testate has no need of

  A. the laws of intestate succession.
  B. a will.
  C. probate.
  D. the laws of accession.

39. Whose signature must be on a deed to make it valid?

  A. the grantee
  B. the grantor
  C. the grantor and the grantee
  D. a notary

40. Extra protection for title problems on property conveyed by a warranty deed is provided by

  A. the acknowledgement.
  B. the signature of the grantee.
  C. the granting clause.
  D. title insurance.

41. The form of deed that carries no warrantees—implied or actual—is a

A. grant deed.
B. quitclaim deed.
C. gift deed.
D. warranty deed.

42. What is the number of the section that is always located in the northeast corner of a township?

A. It is always different.
B. 1
C. 6
D. 36

43. A township in the rectangular survey system always contains

A. 640 acres.
B. 1 square mile.
C. 36 square miles.
D. None of the above—it is not always the same area.

44. Range lines and township lines intersect to create

A. sections.
B. townships.
C. meridians.
D. base lines.

GO ON TO THE NEXT PAGE

Practice Test 3

45. The metes and bounds method of legally describing property dates back to the

    A. Louisiana Purchase.

    B. Northwest Territory Acquisition.

    C. Spanish land grants.

    D. 13 original colonies.

46. Which of the following is not a requirement of a valid real estate sales contract?

    A. acknowledgement

    B. consideration

    C. offer and acceptance

    D. that the contract is in writing

47. Which of the following is correct with respect to making an offer to purchase real estate?

    A. An offeror makes the offer; an offeree receives the offer.

    B. An offeree makes the offer; an offeror receives the offer.

    C. A grantor makes the offer; a grantee receives the offer.

    D. A trustee makes the offer; a trustor receives the offer.

48. An offer to purchase property made by a person under the influence of alcohol is best described as

    A. voidable.

    B. void.

    C. unenforceable.

    D. valid.

49. An offer to purchase real estate is revocable by the person

    A. making the offer.

    B. receiving the offer.

    C. making the offer, as long as the offer is not in writing.

    D. making the offer, as long as no money accompanies the offer.

50. What is the law that requires most real estate contracts to be in writing?

    A. Parol Evidence Law

    B. Truth in Lending Law

    C. Statute of Frauds

    D. Real Estate Settlement and Procedures Act

51. What clause in the original mortgage loan or trust deed would prevent the use of a wraparound mortgage by a seller?

    A. due-on-sale clause

    B. acceleration clause

    C. contingency clause

    D. prepayment penalty clause

52. A security instrument in a loan

    A. hypothecates the property.

    B. subordinates the property.

    C. forecloses the property.

    D. redeems the property.

GO ON TO THE NEXT PAGE

53. In analyzing whether to approve a mortgage loan application, the lender will consider all but which of the following?

    A. the credit history of the borrower

    B. the ethnic background of the borrower

    C. the ability of the property to secure the debt

    D. the employment of the borrower

54. What is the difference between buying property and assuming an existing mortgage or buying the property subject to an existing mortgage?

    A. There is no difference.

    B. The seller is still liable to the lender under the subject to situation.

    C. The seller is still liable to the lender under the assumed mortgage situation.

    D. The buyer is liable to the seller under the subject to situation.

55. A purchaser borrows $275,000 to purchase a property for a term of ten years. At the end of that time, $100,000 of the loan will have been paid off and the borrower will have to make a final payment of $175,000. What is the payment called?

    A. final payment

    B. balloon payment

    C. closing payment

    D. termination payment

56. A loan arrangement that allows payments to be made to a seller who, in turn, continues to make payments on an existing loan is called a(n)

    A. wraparound mortgage.

    B. blanket mortgage.

    C. package mortgage.

    D. all of the above

57. In a case where a borrower pays 2 discount points on a mortgage loan, which of the following is true?

    A. The nominal rate and the APR will be the same.

    B. The nominal rate will be lower than the APR.

    C. The nominal rate will be higher than the APR.

    D. The nominal rate will be higher than the APR but only in an adjustable-rate mortgage loan.

58. Which of the following types of mortgage loans features a monthly payment that does not change throughout the life of the loan?

    A. fixed rate; fully amortized

    B. fixed rate; partially amortized

    C. graduated payment; fully amortized

    D. growing equity; fully amortized

59. The funds for a VA loan are received by the mortgagor from

    A. the Veterans Administration.

    B. the Federal Housing Administartion.

    C. a primary lender

    D. the Department of Housing and Urban Development.

60. The process of dividing up charges, payments, credits, and debits between a buyer and seller at closing is known as

    A. reconciliation.

    B. adjustment.

    C. accounting.

    D. proration.

GO ON TO THE NEXT PAGE

Practice Test 3

61. Which of the following items is typically not charged to a buyer who is already renting the house he is purchasing?

    A. property taxes for the day of closing

    B. interest on an assumed mortgage

    C. rent to the seller for the day of closing

    D. documentary stamp tax on deeds

62. An owner has collected all the rents for his apartment building on February 1 for the month of February. He closes on the sale of the building on February 15. How are the rents prorated, if at all?

    A. The seller gets to keep the rents for the whole month.

    B. The buyer receives the rents for the whole month.

    C. The rents are prorated; the buyer gets a debit and the seller gets a credit as of the date of closing.

    D. The rents are prorated; the buyer gets a credit and the seller gets a debit as of the day of closing.

63. Which of the following is not true about title insurance?

    A. The seller is required to provide title insurance.

    B. Title insurance is always prudent to obtain.

    C. Lenders will normally require title insurance on properties they lend money on.

    D. Buyers' agents should recommend the purchase of title insurance to their buyers.

64. When considering depreciation, the concept of whether an item of physical deterioration is curable or incurable is a function

    A. only of its cost.

    B. only of the value it adds.

    C. of whether the item can actually be corrected.

    D. of its cost relative to the value it adds.

65. Which of the following best describes the type of income used in the income capitalization approach?

A. potential gross income
B. potential rental income
C. scheduled gross income
D. scheduled rental income

66. An appraiser asked to appraise a church would most likely use what valuation approach?

A. income capitalization approach
B. cost approach
C. gross rent multiplier approach
D. sales comparison approach

67. In the sales comparison approach, the value of a feature present in a comparable that is not present in the subject is

A. added to the selling price of the subject.
B. subtracted from the selling price of the subject.
C. added to the selling price of the comparable.
D. subtracted from the selling price of the comparable.

68. Which of the following is not a characteristic of value?

A. demand
B. transferability
C. utility
D. anticipation

GO ON TO THE NEXT PAGE

69. Requirements regarding amperage and wattage would most likely be found in the

    A. building code.
    B. plumbing code.
    C. environmental code.
    D. electrical code.

70. The U.S. Department of Energy has established minimum insulation recommendations according to

    A. county.
    B. state.
    C. census tract.
    D. zip code.

71. Windows characterized by smaller overlapping panes of glass are called

    A. jalousie windows.
    B. casement windows.
    C. awning windows.
    D. hopper windows.

72. Voltage requirements in newer homes is generally

    A. 100 and 150.
    B. 110 and 120.
    C. 110 and 220.
    D. 120 and 240.

73. Money that comes from an investment on an annual basis after all expenses are paid is called

    A. equity.
    B. leverage.
    C. appreciation.
    D. cash flow.

74. The possible loss of invested capital or expected earnings from an investment is best referred to as

    A. liquidity risk.
    B. leverage risk.
    C. purchasing power risk.
    D. safety risk.

75. A way to invest in real estate that is similar to a mutual fund investment is a

    A. limited partnership.
    B. general partnership.
    C. limited liability corporation.
    D. real estate investment trust.

76. Which of the following would not be considered equity?

    A. an investor's cash investment
    B. money belonging to the seller after the sale of a property
    C. funds borrowed through a mortgage loan
    D. value of an investment minus all debts

GO ON TO THE NEXT PAGE

77. Not painting an apartment building that you own when it needs it may be called

    A. deferred maintenance
    B. capital costs
    C. cash flow outlay
    D. functional obsolescence

78. With respect to taxation, a property owned by the government is considered

    A. immune.
    B. exempt.
    C. partially exempt.
    D. relieved.

79. For capital gains purposes, how are capital improvement expenses to a property treated?

    A. They are added to the purchase price.
    B. They are subtracted from the purchase price.
    C. They are ignored with respect to the purchase price.
    D. They are deducted from capital gains taxes owed.

80. Which of the following is most correct about depreciation calculations?

    A. The total purchase price of the property may be depreciated.
    B. The total purchase price of the property plus acquisition costs may be depreciated.
    C. Only the total land value only may be depreciated.
    D. The total purchase price of the property plus acquisition costs minus land value may be depreciated.

81. The Taxpayer Relief Act of 1997 deals with

    A.   investment properties.
    B.   married couples only.
    C.   resident homeowners.
    D.   agricultural properties.

82. The gain realized from the sale of real estate owned for more than one year is generally taxed as

    A.   regular income.
    B.   tax-deferred income.
    C.   capital gain.
    D.   depreciated income.

83. Demand is affected by all of the following except

    A.   availability of mortgage money.
    B.   number of households.
    C.   consumer preferences.
    D.   number of housing units available.

84. Which of the following does not affect the availability of land for construction?

    A.   amount of useable land in a given area
    B.   wetlands ordnances
    C.   zoning
    D.   cost of construction materials

GO ON TO THE NEXT PAGE

Practice Test 3

85. As apartment vacancy rates go down, what usually happens to rents?

    A. They rise.

    B. They fall.

    C. They are unaffected.

    D. The rents for smaller apartments tend to rise, while the rents for larger apartments tend to fall.

86. A person seeking to use property in a way not consistent with the principal uses listed in the zoning ordinance might seek any except which of the following?

    A. a special exception

    B. a variance

    C. a zoning ordinance amendment

    D. a planned unit development

87. Which of the following would not be an appropriate goal for a comprehensive plan?

    A. providing adequate municipal services and infrastructure

    B. protecting property values by appropriately locating incompatible land uses

    C. reducing costs to the community for development

    D. encouraging urban sprawl to reduce infrastructure costs

88. Variances from the zoning ordinance are generally granted by the

    A. city council.

    B. planning commission.

    C. environmental review board.

    D. board of adjustment.

89. Which zoning category does most municipally owned property usually fall under?

    A.   special use
    B.   planned use
    C.   commercial use
    D.   industrial use

90. A shoe factory was built before zoning was adopted by the city. The area in which the shoe factory is located is now zoned residential. The factory is most likely a

    A.   special exception use.
    B.   variance use.
    C.   conditional use.
    D.   nonconforming use.

91. How many acres does the N ½ of the W ½ of the SE ¼ of a section of land contain?

    A.   640 acres
    B.   320 acres
    C.   160 acres
    D.   40 acres

92. A relatively new house contains 2,500 square feet of space. A similar, 2,600-square-foot house built recently cost $338,000 to build, excluding the land costs. What is the estimated reproduction cost of the 2,500-square-foot house?

    A. $338,000
    B. $325,000
    C. $310,000
    D. $300,000

GO ON TO THE NEXT PAGE

93. The estimated reproduction cost of a house is $200,000. The estimated depreciation on the house is 30%. What is the depreciated cost of the house?

    A. $60,000

    B. $140,000

    C. $200,000

    D. $260,000

94. A comparable property sold six months ago for $250,000. Prices of similar properties have increased by 5% since that time. At what amount would a broker doing a competitive market analysis on a similar house likely value the subject property?

    A. $237,500

    B. $250,000

    C. $262,500

    D. $312,500

95. A buyer purchases a property for $260,000 with 100% financing and is required to obtain private mortgage insurance (PMI). Assuming the property's value has not changed, at what point will the buyer be able to stop paying for the PMI?

    A. when he has paid off $130,000

    B. when he has paid off $85,800

    C. when he has paid off $78,000

    D. when he has paid off $65,000

96. What is the first month's interest on a fixed-rate loan at 7% for 25 years for a home that cost $360,000 with an LTV ratio of 80%?

    A. $1,680

    B. $2,100

    C. $20,160

    D. $25,200

97. The total state tax on the recording of a typical new loan to purchase a home for $150,000 outside Dade County would be

A. $300
B. $525
C. $825
D. $1,050

98. Assuming the buyer paid all closing costs, what commission rate was charged if the owner netted $152,737 after paying the commission and the house sold for $161,200?

A. 4.75%
B. 5%
C. 5.25%
D. 5.5%

99. If the monthly payment of principal and interest on a mortgage loan is $1,275, the interest rate is 6% and the original amount of the mortgage is $200,000. What is the principal balance after the first month's payment is made?

A. $198,725
B. $199,725
C. $199,825
D. $199,925

100. How much total interest will a borrower pay on a $250,000, 30-year, fixed-rate, amortized loan at 5%, when the monthly payment is $1,342.50?

A. $12,500
B. $233,300
C. $312,600
D. $375,000

Answer Key 3

Answer Key for Practice Test 3

1. B		**31.** C	
2. C		**32.** B	
3. D		**33.** B	
4. D		**34.** B	
5. D		**35.** B	
6. B		**36.** D	
7. D		**37.** A	
8. B		**38.** A	
9. B		**39.** B	
10. D		**40.** D	
11. A		**41.** B	
12. B		**42.** B	
13. D		**43.** C	
14. D		**44.** B	
15. B		**45.** D	
16. D		**46.** A	
17. D		**47.** A	
18. D		**48.** A	
19. A		**49.** A	
20. B		**50.** C	
21. C		**51.** A	
22. D		**52.** A	
23. B		**53.** B	
24. D		**54.** B	
25. C		**55.** B	
26. B		**56.** A	
27. D		**57.** B	
28. C		**58.** A	
29. C		**59.** C	
30. B		**60.** D	

61. C		**81.** C	
62. D		**82.** C	
63. A		**83.** D	
64. D		**84.** D	
65. A		**85.** A	
66. B		**86.** D	
67. D		**87.** D	
68. D		**88.** D	
69. D		**89.** A	
70. D		**90.** D	
71. A		**91.** D	
72. D		**92.** B	
73. D		**93.** B	
74. D		**94.** C	
75. D		**95.** D	
76. C		**96.** A	
77. A		**97.** C	
78. A		**98.** C	
79. A		**99.** B	
80. D		**100.** B	

Answers and Explanations for Practice Test 3

1. **B.** Membership in the National Association of Realtors is voluntary and only membership entitles the member to use the term *Realtor.*

2. **C.** A separate mortgage broker's license is required to engage in the mortgage business.

3. **D.** This is definitional.

4. **D.** Although the plat map may ultimately be recorded or filed, it is known by this term when it is submitted for approval to the local planning agency.

5. **D.** Clerical employees would not, for example, need a license. Salaried employees not paid on a commission basis would not need a license even if they performed real estate duties.

6. **B.** This is a statutory exemption.

7. **D.** The statutory requirement is passing the law exam.

8. **B.** This is definitional.

9. **B.** This is statutory. Any consumer affairs office (state or local) may become involved in a consumer complaint against a real estate licensee, but the other three agencies are primarily involved in regulation of the industry.

10. **D.** Also, they may only serve a maximum of two consecutive terms.

11. **A.** This is statutory.

12. **B.** This is statutory.

13. **D.** These are some of the agencies involved in real estate licensing.

14. **D.** This is statutory.

15. **B.** A transaction broker provides limited representation to either or both parties but has no fiduciary relationship to either. Dual agency is prohibited by Florida law.

16. **D.** Sales associates will become subagents of brokers in a single agency situation and will owe all fiduciary duties to the principal.

17. **D.** The broker is required to present both offers to the seller as soon as possible.

18. **D.** The no-brokerage relationship might be the only confusing choice, but it also requires disclosure.

19. **A.** A broker in a no-brokerage situation can work with either buyer or seller with no agency representation and can be paid by either party.

20. **B.** This is statutory. The opposite is true of each of the other choices.

21. **C.** Puffing would become false or fraudulent advertising if the statement were untrue as opposed to merely exaggerated.

22. **D.** A board of directors is generally required for a corporation. Trade names are optional. Liability insurance is a good idea but not required.

23. **B.** The tricky answer choice here is commingling, which means mixing client's funds and the broker's own business funds. Conversion occurs if the broker actually uses the client's money for his own interests.

24. **D.** This is statutory.

25. **C.** An informal hearing is held before the commission if the licensee agrees with the charges.

26. **B.** This is statutory.

27. **D.** This is statutory. If you're confused about the fines, remember that this fine would be levied against someone *without* a real estate license. The penalties mentioned in the other questions relate to violations by people who *have* real estate licenses.

28. C. This is historical.

29. C. If the statement were construed to refer to a protected class issue such as race or religion this would be steering. None of the others apply even if the statement were harmless.

30. B. This is statutory. Tenants in older buildings must be allowed to make reasonable modifications to accommodate a handicapping condition.

31. C. This is statutory.

32. B. This is statutory.

33. B. The other forms of ownership can or do have some type of limitation.

34. B. The holder of a life estate has no fee ownership interest but has possession and use.

35. B. Taking title at the same time is a feature of joint tenancy not the other forms mentioned.

36. D. The tricky answer choice here is personal property. A lease is considered personal property, not real estate.

37. A. This is definitional.

38. A. The person who makes a will (testator) and dies testate (with a will) has no need for the laws that deal with the inheritance when someone dies without a will (intestate).

39. B. The person conveying the property (the grantor) must sign the deed.

40. D. Title insurance passes on the liability of the grantor to a title insurance company.

41. B. The quitclaim deed conveys whatever interest the owner has in the property without warranty.

42. B. You don't need a map for this. Just remember that sections within a township are always numbered by starting in the top row on the right (northeast corner) with the number 1 and going left from there.

43. C. Don't get confused with the area of a section, which is 640 acres or 1 square mile.

44. B. Range lines are vertical, township lines are horizontal, and they cross to create townships.

45. D. Historically this is where the metes and bounds description system was first used in this country.

46. A. The acknowledgement is needed to file a deed.

47. A. This is definitional. Choices C and D do not apply to offers.

48. A. The contract may appear to be unenforceable or void, but, technically, when the person is sober, he can affirm the contract and go ahead with the deal or he can decide to void it.

49. A. A normal offer to purchase—even if accompanied by so-called good faith or earnest money—is revocable until accepted and a meeting of the minds is achieved.

50. C. This is statutory.

51. A. The due-on-sale clause requires payment of the mortgage in full at the time of sale. There could be no wraparound mortgage in this case, because the original mortgage would have to be paid off.

52. A. Hypothecation is the pledging of property as security for a loan.

53. B. Credit applicants are protected from discrimination by the Equal Credit Opportunity Act (ECOA).

54. B. "Subject to" does not relieve the seller of liability for the mortgage debt in the event that the buyer defaults.

55. B. Though the other answers may be somewhat descriptive, the final payment is called a *balloon payment.*

56. A. This is definitional. A package mortgage is used when personal property is included with the real estate and a blanket mortgage covers more than one piece of property.

57. B. Discount points are prepaid interest and will result in a lower nominal rate and higher APR.

58. A. The tricky answer choice is B. If the loan is not fully amortized, then the remaining balance is due at the last payment, which means all the payments are not the same.

59. C. Remember that the VA guarantees loans that are made by primary lenders. It does not lend money itself. Also, you must remember that the mortgagor is the person borrowing the money.

60. D. This is definitional.

61. C. If the property were an investment rental property, the buyer would typically be credited with rents for the day of closing; therefore, as a renter, he would not be charged rent. The stamp tax can be negotiated (as all closing date charges can be), but it remains the seller's obligation unless the buyer agrees to pay it.

62. D. The seller collected rents for the whole month but only owned the building for part of the month. The seller owes the buyer that portion of the rents for the time he (the seller) did not own the building. Simply remember that prepaid rents (rents paid before the space is used) are always prorated, with the buyer receiving a credit and the seller receiving a debit, unless otherwise negotiated. Normally, the buyer gets credit for the day of closing.

63. A. This is statutory but may be negotiated.

64. D. Curable and incurable with respect to an item of depreciation has nothing to do with whether the item can actually be repaired. The idea is based on whether the expenditure to repair something would add an equivalent value to the property (curable) or not (incurable). Therefore, cost and value in isolation from each other are incorrect answers.

65. A. Potential gross income is an estimate of market income from all sources including rent, parking, vending, and laundry machines.

66. B. The cost approach is most useful for special-purpose or unique properties where there would be few comparables and no rental income.

67. D. An appraiser never adjusts the subject, so choices A and B can be eliminated. Then remember to ask yourself the question "What do I have to do to the comparable to make it like the subject?" In this case, because the comparable is better, you take away (subtract the value of) the feature.

68. D. Anticipation is an economic principle. The fourth characteristic of value is scarcity.

69. D. This question just makes sure you know that the words *amperage* and *wattage* relate to the electrical service in a structure.

70. D. This is definitional.

71. A. This is definitional.

72. D. These larger voltages are common in newer homes and in many homes built after 1950.

73. D. This is definitional.

74. D. This is definitional and refers to both market risk and risk of default. I made up the term *leverage risk.*

75. D. This is definitional. The three incorrect choices are forms of business organization, which could be used for real estate investments.

76. C. This is definitional. Borrowed funds are never part of equity.

77. A. This is definitional. Capital costs would be expenditures for larger projects like a new roof. There is no such thing as cash flow outlay. Functional obsolescence is a design flaw in the building.

78. A. This is statutory and definitional. Immune properties have no tax obligation and are not assessed.

79. A. Capital expenses are added to the original purchase price to arrive at an adjusted basis.

80. D. In addition to remembering that acquisition costs can be depreciated along with the purchase price, remember that land cannot be depreciated.

81. C. This is one of those "best answer" questions. Under certain circumstances, any of the answers might apply, but the act is primarily designed to relieve resident homeowners of paying excessive capital gains when selling their primary residence.

82. C. This is statutory. Capital gains are usually taxed at a lower rate than regular income.

83. D. Number of housing units available affects supply not demand.

84. D. The cost of construction materials will affect the cost of construction not the availability of land on which to build.

85. A. This is a basic supply and demand question. The fewer apartments that are available, the more rents will rise.

86. D. The planned unit development is a type of large-scale, usually mixed-use development. The other answers are all ways to either get relief from the requirements of a zoning ordinance or in the case of an ordinance amendment, get the zoning changed.

87. D. Good planning as well as Florida's growth management policies discourage urban sprawl. In general, urban sprawl can increase the costs of infrastructure (roads, sewer and water lines, and other municipal services and facilities).

88. D. This is statutory. The board of adjustment is also called the zoning board of adjustment.

89. A. This is definitional.

90. D. The other answers might apply if permission were given to build the factory after the zoning ordinance was adopted. But because the factory preexists correct zoning, it is legally nonconforming.

91. D. In any problem like this, you can ignore the directions and concentrate on the fractions. You'll also have to remember that there are 640 acres in a section. So, $\frac{1}{2} \times \frac{1}{2} \times \frac{1}{4} \times 640$ acres = 40 acres.

92. B. The method for finding this answer is to calculate how much per square foot the second house cost to build and then use that information to estimate the cost of the other house.

$338,000 ÷ 2,600 square feet = $130 per square foot

2,500 square feet × $130 = $325,000

Hint: Don't overthink this question by worrying about economies of scale (that is, that the 2,500-square-foot house would cost slightly more per square foot than the larger house to build). You really don't have enough information to account for that, and at only a 100-square-foot difference, that factor would be negligible or nonexistent.

93. B. You must read this question carefully, because it asks for the depreciated cost of the house, not the amount of depreciation. Also, when a percent of depreciation is given, you must first multiply by that percentage and then subtract that amount from the reproduction/replacement cost.

Reproduction/Replacement Cost – Accrued Depreciation = Depreciated Cost

$200,000 – ($200,000 × 0.30) = $200,000 – $60,000 = $140,000

94. C. This type of problem involves increasing the value of the comparable by the amount of appreciation that has taken place.

$250,000 × 0.05 = $12,500

$250,000 + $12,500 = $262,500

95. D. Generally, PMI may be dropped when 25% of the home's value or mortgage amount has been paid off.

96. A. The term of the mortgage is irrelevant.

$360,000 (Price of House) × 0.80 (LTV) = $288,000 (Mortgage Amount)

$288,000 (Mortgage Amount) × 0.07 = $20,160 (First Year's Interest)

$20,160 (First Year's Interest) ÷ 12 months = $1,680 (First Month's Interest)

97. C. There is a little trick here insofar as, for state mortgage recording tax purposes, whether the property is in or out of Dade County doesn't matter. It does matter for deed recording purposes. You need to remember the recording tax rates: $35 per $100 for the note and 2 mills ($0.002) for the mortgage itself. *Remember:* Mortgage loans generally include the note or promise to pay as well as the mortgage document, which creates the lien on the property.

$150,000 ÷ 100 = 1,500$ units

$1,500 × \$0.35 = \$525$ (Amount for the Note)

$150,000 × 0.002 = \$300$ (Amount for the Mortgage)

$525 + \$300 = \$825$

98. C. First, to find out the dollar amount of the commission, you subtract the net to owner from the selling price.

$161,200 – \$152,737 = \$8,463$ commission

Commission ÷ Selling Price = Commission Rate

$8,463 ÷ \$161,200 = 0.525$ (or 5.25%)

99. B. The thing to remember is that interest is always paid on the unpaid balance and that, for these kinds of problems, annual interest divided by 12 months is a pretty close estimate of the first month's interest payment.

$200,000 (Mortgage Amount) × 0.06 (Annual Interest Rate) = \$12,000$

$12,000 (First Year's Interest) ÷ 12 months = \$1,000$ (First Month's Interest)

$1,275 (Monthly Payment) – \$1,000 (Interest) = \$275$ (Principal Payment)

Remember here that each monthly payment on an amortized mortgage is made up of principal and interest.

$200,000 (Amount of Mortgage) – \$275 (First Month's Principal Payment) = \$199,725$ (Principal Balance Remaining after the First Month's Payment)

100. B. The thing to remember here is that each payment is part principal and part interest and that everything you pay back is interest except for the amount of the original principal. Also the 5% is irrelevant to calculate the answer.

$1,342.50 (Monthly Payment of Principal and Interest) × 12 months × 30 years = \$483,300$ (Total Payments)

$483,300 (Total Payments for the Life of the Loan) – \$250,000 (Original Principal) = \$233,300$ (Interest Paid)

Answer Sheet for Practice Test 4

(Remove This Sheet and Use It to Mark Your Answers.)

1 Ⓐ Ⓑ Ⓒ Ⓓ	21 Ⓐ Ⓑ Ⓒ Ⓓ	41 Ⓐ Ⓑ Ⓒ Ⓓ
2 Ⓐ Ⓑ Ⓒ Ⓓ	22 Ⓐ Ⓑ Ⓒ Ⓓ	42 Ⓐ Ⓑ Ⓒ Ⓓ
3 Ⓐ Ⓑ Ⓒ Ⓓ	23 Ⓐ Ⓑ Ⓒ Ⓓ	43 Ⓐ Ⓑ Ⓒ Ⓓ
4 Ⓐ Ⓑ Ⓒ Ⓓ	24 Ⓐ Ⓑ Ⓒ Ⓓ	44 Ⓐ Ⓑ Ⓒ Ⓓ
5 Ⓐ Ⓑ Ⓒ Ⓓ	25 Ⓐ Ⓑ Ⓒ Ⓓ	45 Ⓐ Ⓑ Ⓒ Ⓓ
6 Ⓐ Ⓑ Ⓒ Ⓓ	26 Ⓐ Ⓑ Ⓒ Ⓓ	46 Ⓐ Ⓑ Ⓒ Ⓓ
7 Ⓐ Ⓑ Ⓒ Ⓓ	27 Ⓐ Ⓑ Ⓒ Ⓓ	47 Ⓐ Ⓑ Ⓒ Ⓓ
8 Ⓐ Ⓑ Ⓒ Ⓓ	28 Ⓐ Ⓑ Ⓒ Ⓓ	48 Ⓐ Ⓑ Ⓒ Ⓓ
9 Ⓐ Ⓑ Ⓒ Ⓓ	29 Ⓐ Ⓑ Ⓒ Ⓓ	49 Ⓐ Ⓑ Ⓒ Ⓓ
10 Ⓐ Ⓑ Ⓒ Ⓓ	30 Ⓐ Ⓑ Ⓒ Ⓓ	50 Ⓐ Ⓑ Ⓒ Ⓓ
11 Ⓐ Ⓑ Ⓒ Ⓓ	31 Ⓐ Ⓑ Ⓒ Ⓓ	51 Ⓐ Ⓑ Ⓒ Ⓓ
12 Ⓐ Ⓑ Ⓒ Ⓓ	32 Ⓐ Ⓑ Ⓒ Ⓓ	52 Ⓐ Ⓑ Ⓒ Ⓓ
13 Ⓐ Ⓑ Ⓒ Ⓓ	33 Ⓐ Ⓑ Ⓒ Ⓓ	53 Ⓐ Ⓑ Ⓒ Ⓓ
14 Ⓐ Ⓑ Ⓒ Ⓓ	34 Ⓐ Ⓑ Ⓒ Ⓓ	54 Ⓐ Ⓑ Ⓒ Ⓓ
15 Ⓐ Ⓑ Ⓒ Ⓓ	35 Ⓐ Ⓑ Ⓒ Ⓓ	55 Ⓐ Ⓑ Ⓒ Ⓓ
16 Ⓐ Ⓑ Ⓒ Ⓓ	36 Ⓐ Ⓑ Ⓒ Ⓓ	56 Ⓐ Ⓑ Ⓒ Ⓓ
17 Ⓐ Ⓑ Ⓒ Ⓓ	37 Ⓐ Ⓑ Ⓒ Ⓓ	57 Ⓐ Ⓑ Ⓒ Ⓓ
18 Ⓐ Ⓑ Ⓒ Ⓓ	38 Ⓐ Ⓑ Ⓒ Ⓓ	58 Ⓐ Ⓑ Ⓒ Ⓓ
19 Ⓐ Ⓑ Ⓒ Ⓓ	39 Ⓐ Ⓑ Ⓒ Ⓓ	59 Ⓐ Ⓑ Ⓒ Ⓓ
20 Ⓐ Ⓑ Ⓒ Ⓓ	40 Ⓐ Ⓑ Ⓒ Ⓓ	60 Ⓐ Ⓑ Ⓒ Ⓓ

61 Ⓐ Ⓑ Ⓒ Ⓓ	81 Ⓐ Ⓑ Ⓒ Ⓓ
62 Ⓐ Ⓑ Ⓒ Ⓓ	82 Ⓐ Ⓑ Ⓒ Ⓓ
63 Ⓐ Ⓑ Ⓒ Ⓓ	83 Ⓐ Ⓑ Ⓒ Ⓓ
64 Ⓐ Ⓑ Ⓒ Ⓓ	84 Ⓐ Ⓑ Ⓒ Ⓓ
65 Ⓐ Ⓑ Ⓒ Ⓓ	85 Ⓐ Ⓑ Ⓒ Ⓓ
66 Ⓐ Ⓑ Ⓒ Ⓓ	86 Ⓐ Ⓑ Ⓒ Ⓓ
67 Ⓐ Ⓑ Ⓒ Ⓓ	87 Ⓐ Ⓑ Ⓒ Ⓓ
68 Ⓐ Ⓑ Ⓒ Ⓓ	88 Ⓐ Ⓑ Ⓒ Ⓓ
69 Ⓐ Ⓑ Ⓒ Ⓓ	89 Ⓐ Ⓑ Ⓒ Ⓓ
70 Ⓐ Ⓑ Ⓒ Ⓓ	90 Ⓐ Ⓑ Ⓒ Ⓓ
71 Ⓐ Ⓑ Ⓒ Ⓓ	91 Ⓐ Ⓑ Ⓒ Ⓓ
72 Ⓐ Ⓑ Ⓒ Ⓓ	92 Ⓐ Ⓑ Ⓒ Ⓓ
73 Ⓐ Ⓑ Ⓒ Ⓓ	93 Ⓐ Ⓑ Ⓒ Ⓓ
74 Ⓐ Ⓑ Ⓒ Ⓓ	94 Ⓐ Ⓑ Ⓒ Ⓓ
75 Ⓐ Ⓑ Ⓒ Ⓓ	95 Ⓐ Ⓑ Ⓒ Ⓓ
76 Ⓐ Ⓑ Ⓒ Ⓓ	96 Ⓐ Ⓑ Ⓒ Ⓓ
77 Ⓐ Ⓑ Ⓒ Ⓓ	97 Ⓐ Ⓑ Ⓒ Ⓓ
78 Ⓐ Ⓑ Ⓒ Ⓓ	98 Ⓐ Ⓑ Ⓒ Ⓓ
79 Ⓐ Ⓑ Ⓒ Ⓓ	99 Ⓐ Ⓑ Ⓒ Ⓓ
80 Ⓐ Ⓑ Ⓒ Ⓓ	100 Ⓐ Ⓑ Ⓒ Ⓓ

CUT HERE

Practice Test 4

1. The term *dedication* is most closely associated with the term

   A. gift.
   B. exchange.
   C. sale.
   D. depreciation.

2. Developers who build several model homes for a buyer's selection to be built in a subdivision are said to be building

   A. custom homes.
   B. tract homes.
   C. spec homes.
   D. modular homes.

3. A business opportunity broker

   A. requires a real estate license.
   B. does not require a real estate license.
   C. requires a real estate license if more than half the business's assets are in real estate.
   D. requires the same expertise as a real estate broker.

4. According to state law, the size of a piece of property to be considered agricultural land is

   A. less than 10 acres.
   B. more than 10 acres.
   C. more than 25 acres.
   D. more than 100 acres.

GO ON TO THE NEXT PAGE

5. A real estate applicant having no prior real estate experience is first licensed as a(n)

    A. Realtor.

    B. broker.

    C. broker associate.

    D. inactive sales associate.

6. A nonresident of the state of Florida

    A. may become a sales associate or broker.

    B. may become a sales associate but not a broker.

    C. may become a sales associate or broker, but must become a resident within 60 days of obtaining her license.

    D. may not become a sales associate or broker until she becomes a resident.

7. Acting as a real estate agent without proper licensing

    A. will be grounds for barring the person from ever obtaining a real estate license.

    B. will be no problem as long as a license is obtained within a year of the unlicensed activity.

    C. may be overlooked in obtaining a real estate license if sufficient time with good behavior has passed since the unlicensed activity.

    D. will not be a problem if the activity by the unlicensed person is conducted under the supervision of a licensed broker.

8. A real estate sales associate must take a

    A. 30-hour post-licensing course within two years of his initial licensing.

    B. 45 hour post-licensing course within four years of his initial licensing.

    C. 45-hour post-licensing course before his first renewal period.

    D. 45-hour post-licensing course before his second renewal period.

9. A person who wants to obtain a broker's license but not open her own brokerage may

    A. register as a broker associate and work for another broker.
    B. register as an active sales associate working for a broker.
    C. register as a broker working for another broker.
    D. not do so under Florida state law.

10. Which of the following individuals must have a real estate license if performing the stated activities for a fee for another person?

    A. a person who arranges property exchanges
    B. a person who rents lots in a mobile home park
    C. salaried employees who work onsite renting apartment units
    D. personal property brokers

11. The experience requirement for a sales associate to become a broker is

    A. one year any time.
    B. two years any time.
    C. one year within the last five years.
    D. two years within the last ten years.

12. If Broker A's license has been suspended, what happens to the sales associates?

    A. They may continue working for three months after the suspension.
    B. They must stop working immediately.
    C. They may continue to work under a special inactive broker's license provision.
    D. Nothing.

GO ON TO THE NEXT PAGE

13. Which of the following advertisements does not result in a real estate school's license being suspended?

   A.   "Pass the state exam or your money back."
   B.   "Special preparation using questions from the state exam."
   C.   "This school is endorsed by the Florida Real Estate Commission."
   D.   "Highest state exam pass rate in the state last year" (assuming the statement is true).

14. Seller A is represented by a real estate broker. Buyer B has no representation in this transaction. Buyer B is considered a

   A.   principal.
   B.   client.
   C.   customer.
   D.   transactional principal.

15. A residential sale in Florida would not include a

   A.   one- to four-family house.
   B.   six-unit garden apartment building.
   C.   5-acre farm.
   D.   15-acre piece of vacant land approved for construction of three houses.

16. When a broker is hired to perform services in a nonrepresentative capacity, which of the following duties is not owed?

   A.   honest and fair dealing
   B.   confidentiality
   C.   accounting
   D.   disclosure of material facts

17. Sales Associate A and Sales Associate B work for the same broker. Sales Associate A takes a listing and is hired as a single agent to sell a house. Sales Associate B is hired as a single agent by a buyer. Sales Associate B shows the listed house to his principal. Which of the following best describes this situation?

A. The broker has automatically become a transaction broker.

B. The sales associates have become designated agents.

C. An illegal dual agency situation is being created.

D. The sale can continue with no change in status.

18. Agency disclosure requirements at an open house

A. are always mandatory.

B. do not exist.

C. exist if an offer is made.

D. are the responsibility of the principal rather than the agent.

19. The relationship that provides the most complete set of duties to a principal is

A. no brokerage.

B. transaction.

C. single agency.

D. dual agency.

20. When buyer and seller make conflicting demands regarding the disbursement of escrow funds, the first thing the broker must do is

A. file a petition with the court.

B. contact the Department of Housing and Urban Development.

C. transmit all the funds to the party making the earlier claim.

D. notify the Florida Real Estate Commission.

GO ON TO THE NEXT PAGE

21. Escrow deposits given to a sales associate must be delivered to the broker by the end of business

    A. the next day after receipt.

    B. the second day after receipt.

    C. the third day after receipt.

    D. the fifth business day after receipt.

22. Brokers who provide information on rental units for a fee must return

    A. the entire fee if the prospective tenant fails to obtain a rental unit.

    B. the entire fee if requested within 60 days.

    C. 75% of the fee if an unsuccessful tenant requests it within 30 days.

    D. no portion of the fees under any circumstances.

23. Deposit of escrow funds with the court pending a decision on disbursement is called

    A. escrowing.

    B. interpleading.

    C. trusting fund creation.

    D. conversion.

24. Criminal penalties for violations of Florida Real Estate License Law

    A. do not exist.

    B. may include a fine.

    C. may include jail time.

    D. B and/or C

25. Which of the following is true about the powers of the Florida Real Estate Commission?

    A. The FREC can order repayment of broker compensation.

    B. The FREC can suspend a broker's license until compensation has been repaid.

    C. The FREC can deny payment of broker compensation.

    D. The FREC can order repayment of broker compensation at three times the amount as a penalty.

26. In order for a person to be compensated by the Florida Real Estate Recovery Fund, which of the following must be true?

    A. The act must have been committed by someone falsely posing as a licensed real estate broker.

    B. The act must have been committed by a licensed broker or sales associate who was the seller or purchaser of the property.

    C. The act must have been committed by a licensed broker or sales associate acting as such.

    D. The act must have involved a real estate licensee acting as a corporate officer selling property.

27. A broker who does not properly supervise her sales associates, resulting in license law violations by those associates, is guilty of

    A. nothing.

    B. concealment.

    C. culpable negligence.

    D. moral turpitude.

28. A resident homeowner of a single-family house refuses to sell his property to an African American. The homeowner claims an exemption from fair housing laws. He is

    A. correct.

    B. correct as long as he does not use a real estate agent.

    C. correct as long as he does not use discriminatory advertising.

    D. incorrect.

GO ON TO THE NEXT PAGE

29. A bank refuses to make loans in a particular geographic area because of declining property values. This practice is

A. acceptable, because bank deposits will be protected.

B. known as redlining.

C. known as blockbusting.

D. known as steering.

30. Which of the following is not exempt from federal fair housing laws?

A. a religious organization

B. a private club

C. a resident single-family homeowner

D. an owner-occupied, five-unit apartment building

31. A borrower is given a special information book, a good faith estimate of closing costs, and a servicing disclosure statement when he applies for a mortgage loan. What law is this in accordance with?

A. Regulation Z

B. Truth in Lending

C. Equal Credit Opportunity Act

D. Real Estate Settlement and Procedures Act

32. Payment of a fee by a mortgage broker to a real estate broker for referring a client is

A. illegal.

B. legal.

C. legal if it is not for the same transaction they are both working on.

D. a license law violation but not illegal.

33. A, B, and C own property as joint tenants. A sells her share to D. What is the new status of the ownership?

   A. B, C, and D are now all joint tenants.

   B. B, C, and D are now all tenants in common.

   C. B and C are tenants in common, and D is a joint tenant.

   D. B and C are joint tenants with each other, and D is a tenant in common with them.

34. In a real estate sale, fixtures

   A. are assumed to stay with the property.

   B. are assumed to go with the seller.

   C. are considered personal property.

   D. must be transferred with a separate bill of sale.

35. Concurrent ownership means

   A. property owned by more than one person at the same time.

   B. property owned by one person.

   C. property owned by individuals one after the other.

   D. property only owned by a married couple.

36. Upon the death of a person who owns property in joint tenancy, her interest goes to

   A. her devisees.

   B. the surviving joint tenants.

   C. her heirs.

   D. any tenants in common.

GO ON TO THE NEXT PAGE

37. The property of a person who dies intestate and with no heirs will be claimed by the state in a process called

    A. escheat.

    B. succession.

    C. devisement.

    D. bequeathing.

38. Which of the following is not a requirement for a valid deed?

    A. the signature of the grantee

    B. that the deed be in writing

    C. a granting clause

    D. a description of the property

39. Owner A buys property near a lake and crosses his neighbor's property every day for more than 20 years to get to the lake. At this point, having never discussed the matter with his neighbor, Owner A has most likely acquired what with respect to his neighbor's property?

    A. ownership by adverse possession

    B. ownership by prescription

    C. easement by prescription

    D. easement by private grant

40. In researching a chain of title on a piece of property being sold, which of the following is true?

    A. The current grantor was the previous grantee.

    B. The current grantee was the previous grantee.

    C. The current grantee was the previous grantor.

    D. The current grantor was the previous grantor.

41. The state needs to build a road across Owner A's property. Owner A refuses to sell. The state could still obtain title to the property by exercising its right of

    A. succession.
    B. escheat.
    C. eminent domain.
    D. public grant.

42. A metes and bounds description starts at a

    A. baseline.
    B. meridian.
    C. point of beginning.
    D. benchmark.

43. What is used to calculate the size of a parcel in the government survey system?

    A. distances
    B. directions
    C. fractions
    D. parcel number

44. Which form of legal description may combine the other forms?

    A. lot and block
    B. metes and bounds
    C. government survey
    D. rectangular survey

GO ON TO THE NEXT PAGE

45. Thirty-six sections best describes a

    A. range.
    B. township.
    C. principal baseline and meridian intersection.
    D. government lot.

46. Buyer A offers to purchase Seller B's house for $400,000. Seller B says he will not accept anything less than $450,000. Buyer A does not respond to the counteroffer one way or the other. After a few weeks go by with no other offers, Seller B contacts Buyer A again and says he will take the $400,000 offered. Which of the following is true?

    A. Buyer A and Seller B have reached a meeting of the minds.
    B. Buyer A must stand by his offer of $400,000.
    C. Buyer A must affirm the $400,000 offer in order for there to be a valid contract.
    D. As long all the previous offers and counteroffers were made in writing, there is mutual assent at this point.

47. Between the date of signing and the date of closing, a real estate sales contract is said to be

    A. executed.
    B. executory.
    C. voidable.
    D. implied.

48. According to Florida law, in order to be valid, listing contracts

    A. must be in writing.
    B. may be in writing, oral, or implied.
    C. must be in writing or oral but not implied.
    D. may be implied or written but not oral.

49. An automatic renewal clause in a Florida real estate listing agreement is

A. never permitted.

B. always permitted.

C. permitted in listing agreements for more than one year.

D. permitted in listing agreements for less than one year.

50. A building contractor cannot finish a project on a house that he agreed to do. The homeowner and the contractor agree that a new contractor will take over the project with terms relieving the original contractor from any further obligation. The agreement with the second contractor is said to be a(n)

A. assignment.

B. novation.

C. assumption.

D. partial completion.

51. The FHA lends money to purchase

A. one-family homes.

B. agricultural properties.

C. commercial properties.

D. none of the above

52. A situation where the balance of the mortgage loan actually increases while payments are being made is called

A. reverse annuity.

B. negative amortization.

C. shared appreciation.

D. growing equity.

GO ON TO THE NEXT PAGE

53. Which of the following terms does not fit with the group referring to a type of mortgage payment plan?

- **A.** nonamortized
- **B.** interest only
- **C.** nonconforming
- **D.** straight note

54. Which of the following is true about FHA loans?

- **A.** They require a prepayment penalty.
- **B.** They do not require mortgage insurance.
- **C.** They have a set interest rate.
- **D.** They require a down payment.

55. The VA loan program will guarantee loans for

- **A.** no more than the CRV.
- **B.** up to 10% more than the CRV.
- **C.** A "reasonable" amount negotiated by the buyer above the CRV.
- **D.** no more than 98.5% of the CRV.

56. Which of the following does not buy mortgages?

- **A.** the secondary market
- **B.** GNMA
- **C.** FNMA
- **D.** FHLMC

57. In seller financing of a home purchase, which of the following is correct?

    A. The seller is the mortgagor; the buyer is the mortgagee.

    B. The seller is the trustee; the buyer is the beneficiary.

    C. The seller is the trustor; the buyer is the trustee.

    D. The seller is the mortgagee; the buyer is the mortgagor.

58. A lender can usually invoke an acceleration clause

    A. if the borrower misses a certain number of payments.

    B. if the buyer tears down the house.

    C. if the buyer fails to pay property taxes.

    D. all of the above

59. In an adjustable-rate mortgage, the number that changes is the

    A. index.

    B. margin.

    C. cap.

    D. ceiling.

60. What type of notice is provided by recording the deed after a closing?

    A. actual notice

    B. lis pendens notice

    C. constructive notice

    D. notice of lien

GO ON TO THE NEXT PAGE

61. A new mortgage from a bank will appear

 A. on the seller's closing statement as a credit.
 B. on the seller's closing statement as a debit.
 C. on the buyer's closing statement as a debit to the buyer.
 D. on the buyer's closing statement as a credit to the buyer.

62. An item paid in arrears is

 A. normally prorated as a credit to the seller and a debit to the buyer.
 B. normally prorated as a debit to the seller and a credit to the buyer.
 C. normally prorated as a credit to both the seller and the buyer.
 D. normally not prorated because the buyer will have to pay the item in the future.

63. Florida state law places primary responsibility for accounting and delivery of funds in connection with a closing on the

 A. attorneys.
 B. escrow agents.
 C. brokers.
 D. sales associates.

64. Net operating income does not include consideration of which of the following?

 A. vacancy rates.
 B. mortgage payments.
 C. operating expenses.
 D. property taxes.

65. The average sales price for your subject property is $300,000, which is 10% below the asking price after three months on the market. The house you are looking at to use as a comparable for your competitive market analysis sold at full asking price, after only two weeks on the market. Is this property a good comparable sale for you to use in your CMA?

    A. Yes, because whatever price a house sells for is its market value.

    B. Yes, because you can adjust for whatever factors are different.

    C. No, because it likely sold below market value.

    D. No, because it sold at asking price.

66. Value can best be described as

    A. value in use.

    B. assessed value.

    C. market value.

    D. value in exchange.

67. Which of the following statements about cost and value is true?

    A. They are always the same.

    B. They are never the same.

    C. They may be the same.

    D. The relationship is described by the principle of conformity.

68. The best definition of an appraisal is a(n)

    A. calculation of value.

    B. estimate of value.

    C. selection of value.

    D. analysis of value.

GO ON TO THE NEXT PAGE

69. The lot that will arguably have the most traffic going past it is the

    A. T lot.

    B. flag lot.

    C. cul-de-sac lot.

    D. corner lot.

70. Pouring the concrete in two separate pours is a characteristic of what type of foundation?

    A. floating slab

    B. monolithic slab

    C. platform

    D. post and beam

71. In order to prevent rot and termite damage, the sole plate will generally be made of

    A. concrete.

    B. cement.

    C. foam board.

    D. pressure-treated lumber.

72. Which of the following gauge wires will be able to carry the most electrical current?

    A. 10

    B. 12

    C. 14

    D. Gauge is not related to current carrying capacity.

73. Which of the following is not considered one of the advantages of investing in real estate?

    A. management
    B. inflation hedge
    C. use of leverage
    D. tax advantages

74. Which of the following is not taken into account when calculating cash flow?

    A. income
    B. operating expenses
    C. mortgage payments
    D. depreciation

75. Notes payable and debts incurred but not yet paid are considered

    A. assets.
    B. liabilities.
    C. capital.
    D. equity.

76. The net value of a corporation would be divided by what in order to ultimately find out how much each shareholder owns?

    A. number of shareholders
    B. number of shares
    C. number of people on the board of directors
    D. number of corporate officers

GO ON TO THE NEXT PAGE

77. The purchase price plus the cost of improvements minus depreciation is a definition of

- **A.** equity.
- **B.** capital.
- **C.** leverage.
- **D.** basis.

78. In order to arrive at taxable value, which of the following is true about the homestead exemption?

- **A.** It is added to the assessed value.
- **B.** It is subtracted from the assessed value.
- **C.** It is added to the market value.
- **D.** It is subtracted from the total value.

79. Current taxes paid on a property

- **A.** are a good indication of what a new owner will pay.
- **B.** should be increased by the consumer price index to estimate what a new owner will pay.
- **C.** should be increased by 3% to indicate what a new owner will pay.
- **D.** are not necessarily a good indication of what new owners will pay.

80. Which of the following is not true about the homestead tax exemption?

- **A.** Applicants must be permanent residents.
- **B.** No more than two homes in the state may qualify at one time.
- **C.** The exemption is $25,000 off the assessed value.
- **D.** Applicants must have title to the property as of January 1.

81. Additional tax exemptions may be available for all but which of the following groups?

    A. all unmarried widows and widowers

    B. all blind persons

    C. all disabled veterans

    D. all persons over 65 years of age

82. In a like-kind real estate exchange, which of the following would not be considered like-kind property for an apartment house?

    A. office building

    B. warehouse

    C. garden apartment complex

    D. none of the above

83. The relationship between demand and price for real estate is

    A. direct.

    B. inverse.

    C. balanced.

    D. unbalanced.

84. If 10% of the units in an apartment building are empty, the building is said to have a

    A. 10% occupancy rate.

    B. 90% vacancy rate.

    C. 10% vacancy rate.

    D. 90/10 vacancy rate.

GO ON TO THE NEXT PAGE

85. When there is an undersupply of housing units relative to demand, the market may be characterized as a(n)

    A. seller's market.
    B. buyer's market.
    C. equilibrium market.
    D. balanced market.

86. Which of the following terms would best describe a project that would impact more than one county?

    A. planned unit development
    B. environmental impact development
    C. development of regional impact
    D. multicounty development

87. What type of relief would be sought by a property owner who wants to build a house closer to the street than the required 50 feet because of a stream running through the back of his property?

    A. plat approval
    B. conditional use permit
    C. rezoning
    D. variance

88. What is the primary goal of the government in controlling nonconforming uses?

    A. to see to it that the owner doesn't lose any money
    B. to maintain an ethnically diverse community
    C. to eventually get the uses converted to conforming uses
    D. to maintain community balance

89. Which of the following is not typically regulated by zoning?

A. size of the lot
B. height of the structure
C. setbacks
D. architectural style of the structure

90. Residential structures in Florida in a special flood hazard area must have their first floors

A. at least 10 feet off the ground.
B. above the 50-year flood line.
C. above the mean high-water mark.
D. above the base flood elevation.

91. If you purchased the northwest quarter of a section of land, what would the length of each side of the property be?

A. 5,280 feet
B. 2,640 feet
C. 1,320 feet
D. 660 feet

92. The local zoning ordinance permits lot coverage by all structures and impervious surfaces of 30%. How many square feet of a lot can be covered if the lot is 150 feet by 250 feet?

A. 3,375 square feet
B. 11,250 square feet
C. 15,675 square feet
D. 37,500 square feet

GO ON TO THE NEXT PAGE

93. The subject property has three bathrooms. A comparable, similar in all other respects to the subject property, has two bathrooms and sold for $235,000. The value of the bathroom is estimated to be $15,000. What is the indicated value of the subject property?

A. $250,000
B. $235,000
C. $220,000
D. $205,000

94. A vacant piece of land measuring 75 feet wide by 100 feet deep sells for $150,000. How much did it sell for per front foot?

A. $2,000
B. $1,500
C. $200
D. $20

95. The comparables location is deemed to be 10% better than the subject location. The comparable recently sold for $350,000. What is the indicated value of the subject property?

A. $365,000
B. $350,000
C. $315,000
D. $300,000

96. A buyer finances the purchase of a $280,000 house with a 100% financing. He must pay PMI until the LTV ratio reaches 75%. Assuming he pays off $10,000 per year on the loan and the house does not appreciate in value, at the end of how many years will he be able to drop the PMI?

A. 3
B. 5
C. 7
D. 8

97. Borrower A must pay 2½ points to secure a mortgage at the rate he wants. The value of the property is $390,000 and the LTV is 80%. How much does he owe the bank in points?

    A. $9,750
    B. $7,800
    C. $6,240
    D. $5,600

98. Real estate taxes of $1,200 are due on a property on January 1 for the previous six months. Sale of the property closes on November 1. What is the proration?

    A. The buyer gets a credit of $800; the seller gets a debit of $400.
    B. The buyer gets a debit of $400; the seller gets a credit of $800.
    C. The buyer gets a credit of $800; the seller gets a debit of $800.
    D. The buyer gets a debit of $800; the seller gets a credit of $800.

99. How much will the state documentary stamp tax be on a note for $155,000?

    A. $542.50
    B. $465.00
    C. $387.50
    D. $310.00

100. If a seller wanted to net $400,000 from the sale of her house after paying a 5% commission, what would the house have to sell for?

    A. $380,000
    B. $400,000
    C. $420,000
    D. $421,053

Answer Key 4

Answer Key for Practice Test 4

1. A		**31.** D	
2. B		**32.** A	
3. A		**33.** D	
4. B		**34.** A	
5. D		**35.** A	
6. A		**36.** B	
7. C		**37.** A	
8. C		**38.** A	
9. A		**39.** C	
10. A		**40.** A	
11. C		**41.** C	
12. B		**42.** C	
13. D		**43.** C	
14. C		**44.** A	
15. B		**45.** B	
16. B		**46.** C	
17. C		**47.** B	
18. C		**48.** B	
19. C		**49.** A	
20. D		**50.** B	
21. A		**51.** D	
22. C		**52.** B	
23. B		**53.** C	
24. D		**54.** D	
25. B		**55.** A	
26. C		**56.** B	
27. C		**57.** D	
28. D		**58.** D	
29. B		**59.** A	
30. D		**60.** C	

61. D		**81.** D	
62. B		**82.** D	
63. C		**83.** B	
64. B		**84.** C	
65. C		**85.** A	
66. D		**86.** C	
67. C		**87.** D	
68. B		**88.** C	
69. D		**89.** D	
70. A		**90.** D	
71. D		**91.** B	
72. A		**92.** B	
73. A		**93.** A	
74. D		**94.** A	
75. B		**95.** C	
76. B		**96.** C	
77. D		**97.** B	
78. B		**98.** C	
79. D		**99.** A	
80. B		**100.** D	

Answers and Explanations for Practice Test 4

1. A. A dedication is the gift of land made by a developer to the appropriate government agency.

2. B. *Tract home* is the term used to describe this type of building.

3. A. This is statutory.

4. B. This is statutory.

5. D. This is statutory.

6. A. This is statutory.

7. C. This will be up to the FREC, and it is part of how the law is administered.

8. C. This is statutory.

9. A. This is statutory.

10. A. This is statutory.

11. C. This is statutory.

12. B. This is statutory.

13. D. Choices A, B, and C are specifically prohibited.

14. C. The customer is generally the third party in the transaction. In this case, the broker and the seller are the first two parties. The customer could be represented by his own broker, in which case he would be that broker's principal. He would still have the customer status with respect to the seller's broker.

15. B. The statutes exclude residential buildings of five or more units from the definition of a residential sale.

16. B. Confidentiality is owed in a fiduciary relationship.

17. C. An illegal dual agency situation is being created, and both buyer and seller must consent to a transition to a transactional brokerage arrangement for the transaction to continue.

18. C. Agency disclosure requirements are generally not an issue at open houses unless an actual offer is made or confidential information is sought from a prospective buyer.

19. C. Single agency provides for all the fiduciary duties to the principal. Dual agency is illegal in Florida.

20. D. This is statutory.

21. A. This is statutory.

22. C. This is statutory.

23. B. This is definitional.

24. D. This is statutory.

25. B. This is statutory. Repayment may be forced by making a condition of license reinstatement after suspension or revocation, but it cannot be ordered directly.

26. C. The fund is designed to compensate people who have been injured monetarily by real estate licensees performing their duties.

27. C. This is definitional within the context of the real estate law.

28. D. There is no exception where race is concerned.

29. B. This is definitional and the practice is illegal.

30. D. This is statutory.

31. D. This is statutory. Choices A and B are essentially the same law.

32. **A.** This is statutory and can result in a fine or imprisonment and payment of triple damages.

33. **D.** In the situation described, C and B remain joint tenants but D becomes a tenant in common as to that share.

34. **A.** Choices B, C, and D all deal with personal property. Fixtures are considered real property.

35. **A.** *Concurrent ownership* refers to ownership by two or more people simultaneously.

36. **B.** Devisees and heirs are essentially the same thing. A person receiving real property through a will is called a *devisee*. A person receiving personal property through a will is called a *legatee*. Both are heirs in relationship to the estate of the decedent.

37. **A.** This is definitional.

38. **A.** The person receiving the property need not sign the deed.

39. **C.** Owner A has acquired a right to use, not own, the property, without the permission of the neighbor.

40. **A.** The current owner who is the grantor (seller) was the buyer (grantee) at some point in the past.

41. **C.** The state, through a suit of condemnation, acquires title by using its right of eminent domain.

42. **C.** Benchmarks might be used to locate a point of beginning but they are generally not included in the description.

43. **C.** In the government or rectangular survey system, a parcel of land is designated by a fraction and a location. The fractions are successive in that they are generally fractions of larger numbers or other fractions. The directions simply indicate the location of the parcel. A description might designate a parcel as the S½ of the SE¼ of a section. If you are being asked to calculate the size of the parcel, you multiply the two fractions by each other and then by 640 acres (the size of a section). The calculation is ½ × ¼ × 640 acres = 80 acres. In calculating area, the directions don't matter.

44. **A.** The lot and block system might have a reference to its location within the government survey lines and use a metes and bounds description for each parcel. You should note that choices C and D are the same, since the government survey system is also called the *rectangular survey system*.

45. **B.** A township consists of 36 sections, each of which is 1 square mile.

46. **C.** As soon as Seller A counteroffered with the $450,000 price, the original $400,000 offer was considered rejected and removed from consideration. The buyer would have to reaffirm this offer for a contract to exist.

47. **B.** Contracts that have terms yet to be fulfilled are said to be executory. They are executed when all the terms have been completed.

48. **B.** This is statutory.

49. **A.** This is statutory.

50. **B.** This is definitional. An assignment would have the original contractor still be liable for the work.

51. **D.** This may be viewed as a trick question, since the FHA does not make purchase loans at all but rather insures loans made by primary lending institutions that are participating FHA-approved lenders.

52. **B.** *Amortization* means paying off the loan as you go. *Reverse* means just the opposite (that is, adding to it).

53. **C.** The other three answers refer to a situation where the balance of the loan is paid off at the end.

54. **D.** FHA loans are not insured for the full value or sales price of the house. Therefore, a small down payment is required.

55. **A.** The buyer can pay more than the Certificate of Reasonable Value, but the program will only insure the CRV amount.

56. **B.** GNMA guarantees that payments will be made to buyers of mortgages but does not actually buy mortgages.

57. **D.** The mortgagor (borrower) gives the mortgage (security document) to the mortgagee (lender). In this case, the seller takes back a mortgage that the buyer gives.

58. D. All these reasons can trigger the acceleration clause, where the lender can demand full payment of the loan immediately.

59. A. The movement of the index is what makes the mortgage adjustable. All the other numbers remain fixed based on the original mortgage/note agreement

60. C. This is definitional. Recording the mortgage documents in effect gives notice of a lien.

61. D. The mortgage money is buyer's money that will be passed on to the seller.

62. B. Items paid in arrears mean they will be paid by the buyer to someone other than the seller. The seller used the property without paying for the period of time that she was in the property. The seller will have to pay the buyer for that period of time. The buyer will get a credit on his statement for the money owed by the seller. The amount owed by the buyer to a third party at some later date will not appear on the statement because it will not be paid at closing.

63. C. This is statutory. Attorneys and escrow agents can be hired to handle closings, and sales associates may actually handle closings on behalf of the brokers, but primary responsibility, according to Florida license law, rests with the broker.

64. B. Mortgage payments are never considered in the net operating income calculation because they relate more to the investor than to the building.

65. C. Though not 100% true all the time, houses that sell in significantly less time than the average house and at a different ratio below the asking price than the average house have often been priced too low in the first place and, therefore, are not representative of market value.

66. D. This question is tricky because market value is what appraisers are estimating *most* of the time—but not *all* the time. The value of something in exchange for something else is a more basic definition of value and, therefore, correct all the time.

67. C. You might be tempted to select Choice D, unless you know what conformity means.

68. B. Although appraisers do many calculations, perform significant analysis of the market, and select comparables and other information, an appraisal is defined as an estimate or opinion of value.

69. D. A corner lot has frontage on two streets, which none of the other lots has.

70. A. This is definitional. Choices C and D are types of framing not foundations.

71. D. The sole plate rests on the concrete foundation. The remaining wood framing is attached to it.

72. A. Although it seems backwards, remember that the smaller the gauge number, the heavier the wire. And the heavier the wire, the more current it can carry.

73. A. The fact that most real estate investments require significant management is not considered an advantage.

74. D. Depreciation is not taken into account because there is no actual payment made for depreciation.

75. B. This is definitional. Other questions in these exams deal with the definitions of the other terms.

76. B. When the value per share is known, then each shareholder's interest would be determined by multiplying the value of one share by the number of shares held.

77. D. The basis is the amount used to calculate capital gains on an investment.

78. B. The homestead exemption is subtracted from the assessed value to arrive at the taxable value.

79. D. Sale of a home will trigger a reassessment which could change the property taxes significantly.

80. B. Only one home at a time may qualify for the homestead exemption.

81. D. Exemptions for people over 65 have an income limitation, so not all may qualify.

82. D. *Like-kind* means real estate for real estate. Use of the property doesn't matter.

83. B. When prices go up, demand goes down. *Inverse* means the two factors under consideration move in opposite directions.

84. C. This is a matter of knowing the terminology for referring to the vacancy rate. This situation could also be referred to as a 90% occupancy rate (not one of the choices).

85. A. Because sellers can demand higher prices for their properties, when there is an undersupply it is called a *seller's market.*

86. C. This is definitional in Florida.

87. D. A variance is a departure from the regulations for a particular lot because of physical hardship.

88. C. You might be fooled by Choice D, but it is too vague to be correct.

89. D. Architectural style is sometimes controlled by deed restrictions.

90. D. This is statutory.

91. B. A section is a square that is 1 mile long on each side. Because there are four quarters in each section, each quarter-section measures ½ mile or 2,640 feet (1 mile = 5,280 feet) on each side.

92. B. The word *impervious* means areas including driveways through which rainwater can't drain. First, you have to calculate the area of the parcel; then you take 30% of that area. Here's the math:

Length × Width = Area

250 feet × 150 feet = 37,500 square feet

37,500 square feet × 0.30 = 11,250 square feet

93. A. If the comparable is worse than the subject, you add the value of the feature to the sale price of the comparable.

$235,000 + $15,000 = $250,000

94. A. Frontage is usually the width across the front of a property along the road. Price per front foot is found by dividing the total cost of the property by the number of front feet.

$150,000 ÷ 75 feet = $2,000 per front foot

95. C. The buyers already paid 10% more to live in the comparable's neighborhood. What would they have paid to live in the subject neighborhood? The answer is 10% less, so 10% is subtracted from the sale price of the comparable.

$350,000 × 0.10 = $35,000

$350,000 − $35,000 = $315,000

96. C. Because there is no appreciation on the value of the property, the loan-to-value ratio (LTV) will reach 75% when the owner pays off 25% of the mortgage loan.

$280,000 × 0.25 = $70,000

$70,000 ÷ $10,000 per year payoff = 7 years

97. B. The key thing to remember is that a point is 1% of the loan amount, not 1% of the value or cost of the property.

$390,000 (Value of Property) × 0.80 (Loan-to-Value Ratio) = $312,000 (Amount of Mortgage Loan)

$312,000 (Loan Value) × 0.025 (Points) = $7,800

98. C. The buyer will be paying the taxes in arrears but not living in the house for the entire six months, so the seller will owe the buyer for the portion of time the seller is in the house. The buyer gets a credit and the seller gets a debit.

$1,200 ÷ 6 months = $200 per month

$200 per month × 4 months (Time Period Seller Was in the House for Which the Buyer Paid the Taxes) = $800 (Credit to Buyer)

Because the buyer paid for the taxes the seller "used," the seller is charged a debit for the same amount.

99. A. You'll have to remember that the tax on notes is $0.35 per $100 of the amount of the note.

$155,000 ÷ $100 = 1,550 units (each of which is taxed at $0.35)

1,550 units × $0.35 = $542.50

100. D. The concept of net to the owner means how much the seller walks away with after paying all expenses after closing. In this case the problem only deals with commission costs. Here's the way percentages work when calculating commissions and selling prices: Commissions are taken away from the selling price—thay are not added to the net-to-owner amount.

$400,000 ÷ 0.95 = $421,053 (rounded).

Why 0.95? If the agent is going to get 5% of the sale price, the owner will get 95%. So $400,000 is 95% of the selling price.

Answer Sheet for Practice Test 5

(Remove This Sheet and Use It to Mark Your Answers.)

1 Ⓐ Ⓑ Ⓒ Ⓓ	21 Ⓐ Ⓑ Ⓒ Ⓓ	41 Ⓐ Ⓑ Ⓒ Ⓓ
2 Ⓐ Ⓑ Ⓒ Ⓓ	22 Ⓐ Ⓑ Ⓒ Ⓓ	42 Ⓐ Ⓑ Ⓒ Ⓓ
3 Ⓐ Ⓑ Ⓒ Ⓓ	23 Ⓐ Ⓑ Ⓒ Ⓓ	43 Ⓐ Ⓑ Ⓒ Ⓓ
4 Ⓐ Ⓑ Ⓒ Ⓓ	24 Ⓐ Ⓑ Ⓒ Ⓓ	44 Ⓐ Ⓑ Ⓒ Ⓓ
5 Ⓐ Ⓑ Ⓒ Ⓓ	25 Ⓐ Ⓑ Ⓒ Ⓓ	45 Ⓐ Ⓑ Ⓒ Ⓓ
6 Ⓐ Ⓑ Ⓒ Ⓓ	26 Ⓐ Ⓑ Ⓒ Ⓓ	46 Ⓐ Ⓑ Ⓒ Ⓓ
7 Ⓐ Ⓑ Ⓒ Ⓓ	27 Ⓐ Ⓑ Ⓒ Ⓓ	47 Ⓐ Ⓑ Ⓒ Ⓓ
8 Ⓐ Ⓑ Ⓒ Ⓓ	28 Ⓐ Ⓑ Ⓒ Ⓓ	48 Ⓐ Ⓑ Ⓒ Ⓓ
9 Ⓐ Ⓑ Ⓒ Ⓓ	29 Ⓐ Ⓑ Ⓒ Ⓓ	49 Ⓐ Ⓑ Ⓒ Ⓓ
10 Ⓐ Ⓑ Ⓒ Ⓓ	30 Ⓐ Ⓑ Ⓒ Ⓓ	50 Ⓐ Ⓑ Ⓒ Ⓓ
11 Ⓐ Ⓑ Ⓒ Ⓓ	31 Ⓐ Ⓑ Ⓒ Ⓓ	51 Ⓐ Ⓑ Ⓒ Ⓓ
12 Ⓐ Ⓑ Ⓒ Ⓓ	32 Ⓐ Ⓑ Ⓒ Ⓓ	52 Ⓐ Ⓑ Ⓒ Ⓓ
13 Ⓐ Ⓑ Ⓒ Ⓓ	33 Ⓐ Ⓑ Ⓒ Ⓓ	53 Ⓐ Ⓑ Ⓒ Ⓓ
14 Ⓐ Ⓑ Ⓒ Ⓓ	34 Ⓐ Ⓑ Ⓒ Ⓓ	54 Ⓐ Ⓑ Ⓒ Ⓓ
15 Ⓐ Ⓑ Ⓒ Ⓓ	35 Ⓐ Ⓑ Ⓒ Ⓓ	55 Ⓐ Ⓑ Ⓒ Ⓓ
16 Ⓐ Ⓑ Ⓒ Ⓓ	36 Ⓐ Ⓑ Ⓒ Ⓓ	56 Ⓐ Ⓑ Ⓒ Ⓓ
17 Ⓐ Ⓑ Ⓒ Ⓓ	37 Ⓐ Ⓑ Ⓒ Ⓓ	57 Ⓐ Ⓑ Ⓒ Ⓓ
18 Ⓐ Ⓑ Ⓒ Ⓓ	38 Ⓐ Ⓑ Ⓒ Ⓓ	58 Ⓐ Ⓑ Ⓒ Ⓓ
19 Ⓐ Ⓑ Ⓒ Ⓓ	39 Ⓐ Ⓑ Ⓒ Ⓓ	59 Ⓐ Ⓑ Ⓒ Ⓓ
20 Ⓐ Ⓑ Ⓒ Ⓓ	40 Ⓐ Ⓑ Ⓒ Ⓓ	60 Ⓐ Ⓑ Ⓒ Ⓓ

61 Ⓐ Ⓑ Ⓒ Ⓓ	81 Ⓐ Ⓑ Ⓒ Ⓓ
62 Ⓐ Ⓑ Ⓒ Ⓓ	82 Ⓐ Ⓑ Ⓒ Ⓓ
63 Ⓐ Ⓑ Ⓒ Ⓓ	83 Ⓐ Ⓑ Ⓒ Ⓓ
64 Ⓐ Ⓑ Ⓒ Ⓓ	84 Ⓐ Ⓑ Ⓒ Ⓓ
65 Ⓐ Ⓑ Ⓒ Ⓓ	85 Ⓐ Ⓑ Ⓒ Ⓓ
66 Ⓐ Ⓑ Ⓒ Ⓓ	86 Ⓐ Ⓑ Ⓒ Ⓓ
67 Ⓐ Ⓑ Ⓒ Ⓓ	87 Ⓐ Ⓑ Ⓒ Ⓓ
68 Ⓐ Ⓑ Ⓒ Ⓓ	88 Ⓐ Ⓑ Ⓒ Ⓓ
69 Ⓐ Ⓑ Ⓒ Ⓓ	89 Ⓐ Ⓑ Ⓒ Ⓓ
70 Ⓐ Ⓑ Ⓒ Ⓓ	90 Ⓐ Ⓑ Ⓒ Ⓓ
71 Ⓐ Ⓑ Ⓒ Ⓓ	91 Ⓐ Ⓑ Ⓒ Ⓓ
72 Ⓐ Ⓑ Ⓒ Ⓓ	92 Ⓐ Ⓑ Ⓒ Ⓓ
73 Ⓐ Ⓑ Ⓒ Ⓓ	93 Ⓐ Ⓑ Ⓒ Ⓓ
74 Ⓐ Ⓑ Ⓒ Ⓓ	94 Ⓐ Ⓑ Ⓒ Ⓓ
75 Ⓐ Ⓑ Ⓒ Ⓓ	95 Ⓐ Ⓑ Ⓒ Ⓓ
76 Ⓐ Ⓑ Ⓒ Ⓓ	96 Ⓐ Ⓑ Ⓒ Ⓓ
77 Ⓐ Ⓑ Ⓒ Ⓓ	97 Ⓐ Ⓑ Ⓒ Ⓓ
78 Ⓐ Ⓑ Ⓒ Ⓓ	98 Ⓐ Ⓑ Ⓒ Ⓓ
79 Ⓐ Ⓑ Ⓒ Ⓓ	99 Ⓐ Ⓑ Ⓒ Ⓓ
80 Ⓐ Ⓑ Ⓒ Ⓓ	100 Ⓐ Ⓑ Ⓒ Ⓓ

CUT HERE

Practice Test 5

Directions: For each of the following questions, select the choice that best answers the question.

1. Streets are often given to a municipality as part of a subdivision. The proper term for this transfer of property is

   A. grant.
   B. transfer.
   C. donation.
   D. dedication.

2. A home built without a contract to a specific buyer is said to be a

   A. tract home.
   B. spec home.
   C. custom home.
   D. creative financed home.

3. The federal government primarily influences the real estate market through

   A. its zoning policy.
   B. its monetary policy.
   C. development of model subdivision regulations.
   D. development of model building codes.

4. Real estate brokers

   A. may only do CMAs.
   B. may do CMAs and appraisals.
   C. may do CMAs and appraisals for federally related transactions for properties over $250,000.
   D. may never do appraisals.

GO ON TO THE NEXT PAGE

5. An inactive sales associate may become active by

  A. opening a place of business.
  B. taking certain post licensing courses.
  C. taking the broker's examination.
  D. finding employment with a broker.

6. A nonresident who wants to obtain a Florida real estate license must

  A. become a resident.
  B. sign a nolo contendere agreement.
  C. sign an irrevocable consent to service agreement.
  D. all of the above

7. A member of the Florida bar who wants to obtain a real estate license as a sales associate is exempt from

  A. all educational requirements.
  B. all pre-license but not post-license educational requirements.
  C. all post-license but not pre-license educational requirements.
  D. no educational requirements.

8. Continuing education requirements are

  A. 14 hours every two years.
  B. 45 hours every four years.
  C. 14 hours plus attendance at one FREC meeting every two years.
  D. waived for brokers having a four-year real estate degree.

9. As long as the following activities are done for a fee for another, which of the following is exempt from requiring a real estate license?

   A. Selling cemetery lots
   B. Auctioning real estate
   C. Providing rental information through lists
   D. Exchanging real estate

10. If a broker's license is suspended, the licenses of his sales associates are automatically

    A. suspended.
    B. revoked.
    C. put on voluntary inactive status.
    D. put on involuntary inactive status.

11. Which of the following may hold multiple real estate licenses?

    A. brokers
    B. broker associates
    C. sales associates
    D. none of the above

12. How long may a license remain in involuntary inactive status before it expires?

    A. six months
    B. one year
    C. two years
    D. indefinitely

GO ON TO THE NEXT PAGE

Practice Test 5

13. A licensee who wants to keep her license but not work in the real estate business may request

    A. temporary suspension status.

    B. voluntary inactive status.

    C. temporary revocation status.

    D. involuntary inactive status.

14. A person hired to actually do all the things that a person can do for himself, such as buy and sell property, is acting as a(n)

    A. special agent.

    B. universal agent.

    C. general agent.

    D. agent without restriction.

15. In a transactional brokerage, the buyer or seller is considered a(n)

    A. customer.

    B. principal.

    C. agent.

    D. fiduciary.

16. The presumptive relationship of a broker in a real estate transaction, unless otherwise specified, is that of a

    A. dual agent.

    B. single agent.

    C. designated agent.

    D. transaction agent.

17. Which of the following covers a situation where a broker is instructed by a principal to not reveal the existence of a faulty heating system in the house?

   A. The broker is bound by the fiduciary obligation of obedience.
   B. The broker must obtain the seller's permission to reveal the information to a buyer.
   C. The broker is bound by the fiduciary obligation of confidentiality.
   D. The broker is not bound in this case, because this is an unlawful order by the seller.

18. Which of the following relationships results in limited representation for the principal or customer?

   A. transaction brokerage
   B. single agent relationship
   C. no brokerage relationship
   D. designated sales associate arrangement

19. One of the duties of a single agent is to obtain a property at the most favorable price for her principal. In the case of a buyer's agent, this would most likely mean a

   A. lower commission.
   B. higher commission.
   C. lower commission—therefore, this rule does not apply to buyers' agents.
   D. None of the above—this does not apply to buyers' agents because the seller will most likely pay the commission.

20. A partner in a limited liability partnership is

   A. protected from all liability.
   B. protected from personal liability resulting from her actions.
   C. protected from liability from her own errors but not her own acts of negligence.
   D. protected from liability resulting from the acts of another partner.

GO ON TO THE NEXT PAGE

Practice Test 5

21. Which of the following is exempt from the Florida Fictitious Name Act regarding registration of trade names?

    A. sole proprietor brokers
    B. brokerage corporations
    C. brokerage partnerships
    D. brokerage limited partnerships

22. Two brokers whose work together would seem to indicate that a partnership exists when it does not have formed a(n)

    A. ostensible partnership.
    B. limited partnership.
    C. limited liability corporation.
    D. temporary partnership.

23. Which terms are related to escrow accounts?

    A. conflicting demand and good faith doubt
    B. commingling and conversion
    C. advance fees and earnest money
    D. all of the above

24. A broker who intentionally lies about some aspect of the property in order get a buyer to purchase the property is guilty of

    A. moral turpitude.
    B. fraud.
    C. conversion.
    D. concealment.

25. Which of the following is true regarding the recovery of money from the Real Estate Recovery Fund by a real estate licensee who has been monetarily injured in a real estate transaction?

A. No recovery of funds is possible.
B. Recovery of funds is possible if the injured licensee was acting in his professional capacity.
C. Recovery of funds is possible if he was injured by another licensee and the injured licensee was not acting in the capacity of a real estate agent.
D. Recovery is possible if the transaction did not involve another real estate licensee.

26. Appeals from a final order after investigation of a complaint against a licensee would be made to the

A. Florida Real Estate Commission.
B. courts.
C. administrative law judge.
D. Probable Cause Panel.

27. In a case where the Secretary of the Department of Business and Professional Regulations believes that it would be dangerous for a licensee to continue practicing real estate during the 30-day period during which a judgment may be appealed, the secretary may order

A. nolo contendere.
B. summary suspension.
C. temporary revocation.
D. a justifiable cause hearing.

28. Which of the following is not a protected class under the federal Fair Housing Act of 1968 as amended in 1988?

A. race
B. marital status
C. gender
D. religion

Practice Test 5

GO ON TO THE NEXT PAGE

163

29. Initial complaints of violations under the Fair Housing Act are made to

    A. HUD.

    B. the federal courts.

    C. the state courts.

    D. the Human Rights Commission.

30. A real estate broker who contacts homeowners and says, "You'd better sell quickly, before the drug dealers move in and destroy property values" might be a case of

    A. blockbusting.

    B. redlining.

    C. steering.

    D. farming.

31. Which of the following is true regarding affiliated business arrangements?

    A. The person referred must use the affiliate.

    B. The person referred does not have to use the affiliate.

    C. A disclosure of the affiliate relationship is not required.

    D. It is illegal for a broker to refer a client to an affiliate.

32. Which of the following is true regarding the purchase of title insurance?

    A. The seller can require the buyer to use a certain title insurance company.

    B. The lender can require the buyer to use a certain title insurance company.

    C. The lender can require the seller to pay for the title insurance.

    D. The buyer may choose his own title insurance company if he's paying for it.

33. Which unity is common to both joint tenants and tenants in common?

   A.   possession

   B.   time

   C.   title

   D.   interest

34. Which pair of terms is most closely related?

   A.   fee simple absolute and fee simple defeasible

   B.   fee simple absolute and fee simple qualified

   C.   fee simple qualified and fee simple defeasible

   D.   fee simple absolute and life estate

35. A allows B to use A's property as long as C is alive. This is most likely

   A.   a life estate.

   B.   a lease.

   C.   a fee simple conveyance.

   D.   no transfer of any type of property.

36. Which of the following is true about ownership in severalty?

   A.   It involves more than one person.

   B.   It is a form of concurrent ownership.

   C.   Another term for it is *sole ownership.*

   D.   It is the same as fee simple absolute ownership.

GO ON TO THE NEXT PAGE

37. Which of the following is not a requirement for a valid deed?

    A. acknowledgement

    B. grantor's signature

    C. delivery and acceptance

    D. granting clause

38. During the statutory period required to claim ownership by adverse possession, which of the following is true?

    A. The claimant's occupancy of the property must be unknown to anyone.

    B. The claimant pays the taxes.

    C. The claimant must have the owner's permission to occupy the land.

    D. The claimant must have occupied the property for a total of five years out of seven, the time period not necessarily being continuous.

39. Which of the following is correct?

    A. The landlord is the lessor who has a leasehold interest.

    B. The landlord is the lessee who has the leased fee interest.

    C. The tenant is the lessor who has the leased fee interest.

    D. The tenant is the lessee who has the leasehold interest.

40. The requirement that a lease be in writing applies to all

    A. leases.

    B. residential leases.

    C. commercial leases.

    D. leases for longer than one year.

41. How many acres are contained in the standard section directly north of section number 16.

    A. 640 acres

    B. 320 acres

    C. 160 acres

    D. Not enough information is provided.

42. How large is a township in the government survey system?

    A. 36 square miles

    B. 24 square miles

    C. 1 square mile

    D. 640 acres

43. A property description referring to nothing but compass direction in degrees, minutes, and seconds with various distances is most likely a(n)

    A. government survey system description.

    B. plat map description.

    C. metes and bounds description.

    D. assessor's parcel description.

44. In a township, which section is located immediately southwest of section 22?

    A. 15

    B. 23

    C. 27

    D. 28

GO ON TO THE NEXT PAGE

45. An irregularly shaped single lot in a subdivision will most likely be described on a map using the

    A. rectangular survey system.
    B. assessor' parcel number.
    C. metes and bounds system.
    D. government survey system.

46. A broker has signed a sales contract to purchase a home on behalf of a buyer. The broker

    A. is most likely acting in accordance with a buyer agency agreement.
    B. can only do this if the buyer has signed a power of attorney document.
    C. can never do this under any circumstances.
    D. can do this as long as the buyer confirms the agreement within 72 hours.

47. A broker agrees to sell a property on behalf of a seller. The seller wants to come away from the deal with $300,000 and agrees that the broker can keep whatever about of money she is able to sell the property for above the $300,000. This is called a(n)

    A. open listing.
    B. option listing.
    C. net listing.
    D. closed listing.

48. The parties to a real estate contract agree that if the buyer defaults on the contract, the seller will keep the earnest money deposit as full compensation for breaking the contract. This is known as

    A. specific performance.
    B. compensatory damages.
    C. rescission.
    D. liquidated damages.

49. A seller who wants to reserve the right to sell her property herself without paying a real estate commission would want to enter into all but which of the following?

A. an open listing
B. an exclusive agency listing
C. an exclusive right of sale listing
D. an open net listing

50. The procuring cause in a real estate transaction can most correctly be defined as the person who

A. causes the listing agreement to be signed.
B. brings the buyer to the sale.
C. makes the first offer to purchase.
D. arranges for the closing of title to the property.

51. Which of the following is not true about a biweekly mortgage loan compared to a monthly payment loan?

A. The interest rate is lower.
B. The principal is paid back faster.
C. The total interest paid is less.
D. More payments per year are required.

52. Banks who lend money for mortgage loans are practicing

A. disintermediation.
B. intermediation.
C. subordination.
D. amortization.

GO ON TO THE NEXT PAGE

53. The right of equitable redemption in Florida ends

    A. when mortgage payments have been missed for six months.

    B. when foreclosure proceedings begin.

    C. when the property is sold in foreclosure.

    D. one year after the foreclosure sale.

54. The higher the loan-to-value ratio,

    A. the higher the interest rate.

    B. the longer the term of the loan.

    C. the higher the down payment.

    D. the lower the down payment.

55. A foreclosure proceeding is stopped by payment of all the money due, and the loan resumes according to the original terms. The mortgage agreement most likely had what type of clause in it that allows this to happen?

    A. defeasance clause

    B. due on sale clause

    C. acceleration clause

    D. right to reinstate clause

56. A seller takes back a mortgage on a property she sells. The buyer now wants to borrow money from a bank to build a house on the property. The bank, wanting to be in first position, requires the

    A. borrower to execute a subordination agreement.

    B. original seller to execute a subordination agreement.

    C. builder to execute a subordination agreement.

    D. all of the above

57. An estoppel certificate

    A. stops a foreclosure sale.

    B. certifies the unpaid mortgage balance to the new mortgage holder.

    C. requires immediate payment of the mortgage balance due.

    D. stops the sale of a mortgage to another lender.

58. A mortgage satisfaction is provided by

    A. the mortgagor to the mortgagee.

    B. the mortgagee to the mortgagor.

    C. the title company to the lender.

    D. the office of public records to the lender.

59. Financing provided by the seller as part of the buyer's purchase price is called a

    A. purchase money mortgage.

    B. blanket mortgage.

    C. takeout loan.

    D. package mortgage.

60. Which of the following charges would normally appear on both buyer and seller closing statements as a prorated item rather than on only one of the closing statements?

    A. broker's commission

    B. document preparation fees

    C. recording fees

    D. interest on an assumed mortgage

GO ON TO THE NEXT PAGE

61. A prepaid item will appear on

    A. the seller's closing statement as a credit.
    B. the seller's closing statement as a debit.
    C. the buyer's closing statement only.
    D. the buyer's closing statement as a credit.

62. Which of the following is not a state tax charged in connection with a home purchase?

    A. documentary deed tax
    B. documentary note tax
    C. intangible tax on new mortgages
    D. intangible tax on previously recorded assumed mortgages

63. The buyer's deposit is entered on the closing statements as a

    A. credit to the buyer.
    B. debit to the buyer.
    C. credit to the buyer and a debit to the seller.
    D. credit to the seller and a debit to the buyer.

64. The term *reconciliation* in appraising is best described as

    A. averaging the various values.
    B. weighted analysis of the various values.
    C. fitting one of the values to the sale price.
    D. estimating the value.

65. Potential gross income minus a vacancy and collection loss is

   A. scheduled income.

   B. net operating income.

   C. cash flow.

   D. effective gross income.

66. The most probable price a well informed buyer would pay for a property that has been on the market for a reasonable period of time is a good definition of

   A. appraised value.

   B. investment value.

   C. market value.

   D. value in use.

67. What is the formula for calculating value using the income capitalization approach?

   A. Effective Gross Income ÷ Capitalization Rate = Value

   B. Gross Rent × Gross Rent Multiplier = Value

   C. Potential Gross Rent ÷ Capitalization Rate = Value

   D. Net Operating Income ÷ Capitalization Rate = Value

68. A foreclosure sale would most likely result in a sale of property for its

   A. assessed value.

   B. going concern value.

   C. salvage value.

   D. liquidation value.

GO ON TO THE NEXT PAGE

69. Zoning that permits construction to the boundaries of a lot is referred to as

    A.   flag lot construction.

    B.   T lot construction.

    C.   interior lot construction.

    D.   zero lot line construction.

70. The term *potable* is associated with

    A.   sewage.

    B.   insulation.

    C.   drinking water.

    D.   foundation material.

71. An air conditioning unit with a 1-ton capacity is equivalent to

    A.   12,000 BTUs.

    B.   10,000 BTUs.

    C.   6,000 BTUs.

    D.   3,000 BTUs.

72. The amount of energy an electrical device uses is measured in

    A.   volts.

    B.   amps.

    C.   watts.

    D.   volts times watts.

73. Which of the following would not be considered an intangible asset of a business?

    A.   office furniture
    B.   copyrights
    C.   patents
    D.   goodwill

74. All other things being equal, the higher the loan-to-value ratio,

    A.   the lower the interest rate.
    B.   the higher the mortgage payment.
    C.   the lower the mortgage payment.
    D.   the higher the equity.

75. Sale of a large business involving corporate stock is usually handled by

    A.   real estate brokers.
    B.   business opportunity brokers.
    C.   business enterprise brokers.
    D.   stock brokers.

76. Service industries like banks would be considered

    A.   economic base facilities.
    B.   destination properties.
    C.   origin properties.
    D.   export activities.

GO ON TO THE NEXT PAGE

77. What techniques for analyzing the value of a business consider the value of the inventory on hand, the ability to pay off debt, and the value of stock?

   A. liquidation analysis
   B. sales comparison approach
   C. income capitalization approach
   D. replacement cost and depreciation analysis

78. For tax purposes, properties belonging to churches are deemed to be

   A. immune.
   B. exempt.
   C. partially exempt.
   D. obligated to pay.

79. The court proceeding to review taxes for possible adjustment is known as

   A. valuation appeal.
   B. nolo contendere.
   C. certiorari.
   D. assessment review.

80. The Save Our Homes Amendment limits annual increases in assessment to

   A. 3%.
   B. the annual consumer price index (CPI) percentage increase.
   C. 3% or the annual CPI percentage change, whichever is greater.
   D. 3% or the annual CPI percentage change, whichever is less.

81. Any money or personal property included in a like-kind property exchange in order to even out the exchange of properties of different prices is called

A. boot.
B. difference.
C. basis.
D. deferred value.

82. Which of the following is not true about capital gains or losses?

A. Taxes can be eliminated with a like-kind exchange.
B. Long-term gains are taxed at a preferred rate.
C. Capital losses may be deducted against other capital losses.
D. Installment sales stretch out capital gains for a number of years.

83. What effect will a decrease in average household size have on the real estate market?

A. It will increase supply.
B. It will increase demand.
C. It will have no effect.
D. The effect cannot be measured in supply-and-demand terms.

84. Which of the following will not have an effect on supply with respect to real estate?

A. amount of immigration
B. availability of land
C. lower interest rates for construction loans
D. availability of building materials

GO ON TO THE NEXT PAGE

85. When discussing real estate, *situs* generally refers to the property's

A. indestructibility.
B. location.
C. uniqueness.
D. government controls.

86. Which of the following is not typically a way to eliminate a nonconforming use?

A. Take the property by eminent domain.
B. Limit repairs to maintenance and safety items.
C. Prohibit rebuilding if the building is totally destroyed.
D. Limit the time the nonconforming use can exist.

87. Which of the following would most likely be considered a base industry?

A. dry cleaner
B. grocery store
C. computer manufacturer
D. beauty shop

88. As part of comprehensive planning, a community will inventory and locate things like residential areas, agricultural areas, and commercial areas. This type of study is generally called a

A. land use study.
B. demographic study.
C. thoroughfare study.
D. physiographic study.

89. Which of the following is usually not under the control of the local planning commission?

   A. site plan approval
   B. subdivision plat approval
   C. zoning
   D. sign control

90. Higher-than-normal densities of residential use, mixed land uses, and more flexible designs requiring stricter approvals are typical characteristics of a

   A. planned unit development.
   B. special plat subdivision.
   C. development of regional impact.
   D. special use development.

91. A seller closes on his property on December 15. He has paid his taxes for the year on November 15. What, if any, is the proration?

   A. There is no proration, because the closing was in the same calendar year.
   B. The buyer gets a credit and the seller gets a debit.
   C. The buyer gets a credit and there is no charge to the seller.
   D. The buyer gets a debit and the seller gets a credit.

92. The zoning on a commercial lot permits coverage of 20% of the lot with a structure no greater than five stories in height. What is the maximum square footage that can be built on a 350-x-250-foot lot.

   A. 87,500
   B. 17,500
   C. 6,000
   D. 1,200

GO ON TO THE NEXT PAGE

93. A house closed on April 12 and the buyer assumed a mortgage. The interest owed on the mortgage for the month of April was $1,200. How was the interest prorated?

A. The seller got a credit for $1,200; the buyer got a debit for $1,200.

B. The buyer got a credit for $1,200; there is no charge to the seller.

C. The buyer got a credit for $760; the seller got a credit for $760.

D. The buyer got a credit for $440; the seller got a debit for $440.

94. The sale price of a four-unit residential property was $450,000. Each unit rents for $900 per month. Using the gross rent multiplier approach and the information provided, what would be the value of a similar building where each of the four units rents for $750 per month?

A. $475,000

B. $425,000

C. $375,000

D. $350,000

95. A building has a replacement cost of $150,000 and an estimated economic life of 50 years. What is the annual amount of depreciation?

A. $3,000

B. $4,500

C. $5,000

D. $6,000

96. An investment property has a net operating income of $47,700 per year. Buildings of this type are selling at a rate of return of 9%. What is the estimated value of the building?

A. $530,000

B. $524,175

C. $470,700

D. $429,300

97. The reproduction cost of a building is $280,000. Accrued depreciation is estimated at $60,000. The estimated land value is $70,000. What is the estimated value of the property?

    A. $410,000
    B. $340,000
    C. $290,000
    D. $220,000

98. A comparable property sold three months ago for $280,000. Prices in the area have increased 5% in the past six months. What is the indicated value of a similar property?

    A. $294,000
    B. $287,000
    C. $273,000
    D. $266,000

99. What is the market value of a property that is assessed at 60% of market value if the assessed value is $56,500?

    A. $141,250
    B. $94,167
    C. 33,900
    D. 22,600

100. What is the net operating income on a property whose monthly potential gross income is $3,000 if annual expenses are as follows: operating expenses, $10,500; debt service, $13,550; and reserves for replacement, $1,200.

    A. $896
    B. $10,750
    C. $11950
    D. $24,300

Answer Key 5

Answer Key for Practice Test 5

1. D		**31.** B	
2. B		**32.** D	
3. B		**33.** A	
4. B		**34.** C	
5. D		**35.** A	
6. C		**36.** C	
7. B		**37.** A	
8. A		**38.** B	
9. A		**39.** D	
10. D		**40.** D	
11. A		**41.** A	
12. C		**42.** A	
13. B		**43.** C	
14. B		**44.** D	
15. A		**45.** C	
16. D		**46.** B	
17. D		**47.** C	
18. A		**48.** D	
19. A		**49.** C	
20. D		**50.** B	
21. A		**51.** A	
22. A		**52.** B	
23. D		**53.** C	
24. B		**54.** D	
25. C		**55.** D	
26. B		**56.** B	
27. B		**57.** B	
28. B		**58.** B	
29. A		**59.** A	
30. D		**60.** D	

61. A
62. D
63. A
64. B
65. D
66. C
67. D
68. D
69. D
70. C
71. A
72. C
73. A
74. B
75. C
76. B
77. A
78. B
79. C
80. D

81. A
82. A
83. B
84. A
85. B
86. A
87. C
88. A
89. C
90. A
91. D
92. A
93. D
94. C
95. A
96. A
97. C
98. B
99. B
100. D

Answers and Explanations for Practice Test 5

1. D. The other terms may be descriptively correct, but the proper term is *dedication*.

2. B. This is definitional.

3. B. The federal government can develop model codes but does not do zoning. Its most important function (of the choices provided) is its monetary policy because of the impact on mortgage lending.

4. B. Brokers may do appraisals but may not say that they are state licensed or certified appraisers. The law requires licensed or certified appraisers to do appraisals for federally related transactions for properties over $250,000.

5. D. This is statutory and the employment association must be filed with the Division of Real Estate.

6. C. This is statutory.

7. B. This is statutory.

8. A. This is statutory.

9. A. Of this list, selling cemetery lots is the only exempt activity.

10. D. This is statutory. The possible trick in this question is that, if the sales associates were involved in the wrongdoing, their licenses might be suspended, but this would not be automatic.

11. A. Only brokers may hold multiple real estate licenses.

12. C. This is statutory.

13. B. This is statutory.

14. B. This is definitional. There is no such thing as agent without restriction.

15. A. This is statutory. In transactional brokerage, the broker provides limited representation but does not act as an agent and no fiduciary relationship is established.

16. D. This is statutory.

17. D. Obedience in a fiduciary relationship is limited to lawful orders. This is a material fact that the broker is obligated to disclose.

18. A. Only the transaction brokerage arrangement provides for limited representation. The no-brokerage relationship does not provide any representation. The other two choices provide for full representation.

19. A. An agent must represent her principal's interest above all others even against the agent's own interests. Fiduciary responsibility does not follow the source of the payment, so even if the seller is paying the buyer's agent, the agent owes the buyer her best efforts to obtain the property at the lowest price.

20. D. This is statutory.

21. A. This is statutory.

22. A. They have formed an ostensible partnership, which is considered fraudulent.

23. D. All of these terms are related to escrow account funds and how they are handled. The student should have a basic knowledge of each term.

24. B. This is definitional within the law. Concealment is not speaking when the broker should to reveal some important information.

25. C. This is statutory. The point is that a real estate licensee can recover money from the fund if he was injured by another licensee, as long as the injured party was not acting in his role as a real estate agent but only as a buyer or seller. The fund also provides for claims involving escrow account issues.

26. B. Appeals are filed with the court with notification to the Department of Business and Professional Regulation.

27. B. This is statutory and allows the commission to immediately suspend the license instead of waiting the normal 30 days for the order to take effect.

185

28. B. Marital status is not a protected class. Familial status (that is, the presence of children in the family) is a protected class.

29. A. Initially, complaints are made to the federal Department of Housing and Urban Development, but they may eventually be heard in federal court.

30. D. Although one would probably not use scare tactics like this to obtain listings, the point of the question is that blockbusting is only an issue if a protected class is used to generate fear. Drug dealers are not a protected class.

31. B. A broker may refer someone to an affiliate but must disclose the relationship and inform the person referred that he does not need to use the affiliate.

32. D. The lender will usually require title insurance. Who pays for it is negotiable and the seller can choose the company if he pays for it.

33. A. The other three unities are only features of joint tenancy.

34. C. Both these terms refer to the fact that there is a condition with respect to the use of the property that could cause a loss of ownership.

35. A. A life estate can be for the lifetime of the holder of the life estate or another person.

36. C. Choice D might appear correct, except ownership in severalty could be fee simple qualified if there is a condition on the ownership.

37. A. The acknowledgement is necessary to record the deed but is not necessary to make it valid.

38. B. The opposite is true of each of the incorrect answers.

39. D. The landlord is the lessor and has the leased fee interest.

40. D. This is statutory.

41. A. This is a bit of a trick question. All standard sections in a township contain 640 acres.

42. A. A township is square 6 miles on each side and contains 36 sections.

43. C. This is definitional.

44. D. You'll probably have to draw the sections in a township to answer this question. Numbering starts in the upper-right-hand corner, moving right to left then left to right in the next row down, and alternating thereafter. You'll also have to remember your directions with the convention of north to the top, south to the bottom, east to the right, and west to the left.

6	5	4	3	2	1
7	8	9	10	11	12
18	17	16	15	14	13
19	20	21	22	23	24
30	29	28	27	26	25
31	32	33	34	35	36

45. C. A more difficult choice would have been if the lot and block system was included as one of the possible answers. Remember the lot and block description is the description included in the deed but a metes and bounds description will be provided on the filed map for each parcel.

46. B. Brokers cannot sign documents on behalf of a buyer or seller unless specifically authorized to do so.

47. C. This is definitional and the situation as described is an example of this type of listing.

48. D. This is definitional. Compensatory damages would be for actual costs incurred because of the contract breach. Recission would either be an agreement to rescind the contract or sue for its rescission. Specific performance would be to try to force the sale.

49. C. This is definitional. The open net listing is nothing more than an open listing using the net listing method to calculate the broker's fee.

50. B. This is definitional and common practice. The listing broker may not necessarily be the procuring cause of the sale even though he may be entitled to a commission for listing the property.

51. A. The interest rate does not change for a biweekly mortgage, but all the other answers are correct.

52. B. This is really a vocabulary question requiring you to know the meaning of all the terms. *Intermediation* means acting as the middleman, in this case, between depositors and borrowers.

53. C. This is statutory.

54. D. A higher loan-to-value ratio means that the lender is willing to lend a person more with respect to the value of the property, resulting in a lower down payment.

55. D. The right to reinstate after payment of all money due before a foreclosure sale would allow the loan to return to its original terms of payment.

56. B. The subordination agreement voluntarily moves a lender to a subordinate (lower) position so the original seller who holds the mortgage must sign the agreement.

57. B. This is definitional.

58. B. The mortgagee (lender) provides this to the mortgagor (borrower) to indicate that the mortgage loan has been paid off.

59. A. This is definitional.

60. D. The other choices would only appear on the statement of the person owing the fee—either buyer or seller but not both.

61. A. A prepaid item is one that has already been paid before closing so it has been paid by the seller and, therefore, is a credit to him. It appears as a debit to the buyer.

62. D. This is statutory, although individual counties may charge for previously recorded mortgages.

63. A. The buyer has already paid this money so he gets a credit. It is not entered on the seller's statement. The seller's credit against which the deposit will be paid is the total sales price of the property.

64. B. Reconciliation is the process by which appraisers analyze the values arrived at through the three appraisal methods and then give each of them appropriate weight in order to arrive at a final value conclusion. The three values are never averaged to come up with a final value.

65. D. The second step in reconstructing an income and expense statement is to subtract the vacancy and collection loss from potential gross income to arrive at effective gross income.

66. C. This is the usual wording in a definition of market value. Remember that an appraisal sometimes is done for some other value other than market value.

67. D. The income capitalization approach uses the net operating income to calculate value.

68. D. Liquidation value is a value that is related to a quick sale or a sale under special circumstances like a foreclosure.

69. D. Zero lot line refers to the absence of setbacks, which allows construction to the edge of the property boundary.

70. C. The term *potable* refers to the purity of water for drinking.

71. A. BTU means British Thermal Unit. It is a measure of heating or cooling capacity.

72. C. This is definitional.

73. A. Office furniture would be considered personal property.

74. B. A higher loan-to-value ratio means a larger mortgage loan, so a higher payment.

75. C. Business opportunity brokers generally handle the sale of a smaller business.

76. B. This is definitional. Economic base properties bring money into the community, as do origin properties and export activities.

77. A. This is definitional.

78. B. Technically, churches are subject to taxation but are relieved of the obligation to pay by law.

79. C. This is definitional.

80. D. This is statutory.

81. A. This is definitional. Taxes are usually due on the boot amount when the exchange occurs and payable by the person who receives the boot.

82. A. You have to read these choices very carefully. A like-kind exchange does not eliminate capital gains taxes—it defers them to a later date.

83. B. Demand will likely increase because more people will be setting up their own households rather than living in extended families.

84. A. The amount of immigration will have an effect on demand not supply.

85. B. This is definitional.

86. A. With respect to Choice C, the prohibition on reconstruction is often if the building is destroyed by more than 50%.

87. C. Base industries are those that attract outside money to a community rather than recirculate existing money. It is unlikely that all the computers manufactured would be purchased within one community. The other choices are service industries.

88. A. This is definitional. Demographic studies deal with population. Thoroughfare studies analyze traffic circulation issues. Physiographic studies look at soil and drainage conditions.

89. C. Zoning is generally under the control of the principal elected body of a municipality such as the city council.

90. A. This is definitional. Choices B and D are made-up answers.

91. D. The taxes have been paid by the seller for the entire calendar year, but the seller will not own the property for the last 15 days of the year. The buyer must reimburse the seller for those 15 days of taxes. The seller gets a credit; the buyer gets a debit.

92. A. First, you calculate the total area of the lot:

350 feet × 250 feet = 87,500 square feet

Then you calculate the area allowed to be covered (20%):

87,500 square feet × 0.20 = 17,500 square feet

Then you multiply by the five-story height of the building:

17,500 square feet × 5 stories = 87,500 square feet

93. D. The thing to remember about mortgage interest on assumed mortgages is that interest is paid monthly in arrears (at the end of the month for that month). The interest calculation is made using the actual days of the month. The buyer owes the interest for the day of closing.

In this problem:

$1,200 (monthly interest) ÷ 30 days = $40 per day interest

The seller owned the property for 11 days.

11 × $40 = $440 interest owed by the seller to the buyer, because the buyer will have to pay the entire month's interest at the end of the month.

94. C. First, you should calculate the total gross rent of the comparison building:

4 units × $900 per unit = $3,600 gross rent

Then you need to find the gross rent multiplier:

Sale Price ÷ Gross Rent = Gross Rent Multiplier

$450,000 ÷ $3,600 = 125

Then, to get the value of the building you're interested in, you use the following formula:

Gross Rent × Gross Rent Multiplier = Value

($750 × 4 units) × 125 = $375,000

$3,000 × 125 = $375,000

95. A. Here's the formula:

Replacement/Reproduction Cost ÷ Economic Life = Annual Amount of Depreciation

$150,000 ÷ 50 years = $3,000

96. A. This problem requires the use of the formula for the income capitalization approach:

Net Operating Income ÷ Capitalization Rate = Value

$47,700 ÷ 0.09 = $530,000

97. C. This question requires you to remember the cost approach formula:

Reproduction/Replacement Cost − Accrued Depreciation + Land Value = Property Value

$280,000 − $60,000 + $70,000 = $290,000

98. B. Increases in value over time are added to the comparable. This problem requires you to use only three months' appreciation, which is half of the 5% appreciation over the past six months.

5% ÷ 2 = 2.5%

$280,000 × 0.025 = $7,000

$280,000 + $7,000 = $287,000

99. B. Here's the formula:

$56,500 ÷ 0.60 = $94,167

100. D. Net operating income is always calculated using annual numbers, so don't forget to multiply the monthly potential gross income by 12.

$3,000 × 12 = $36,000

$36,000 − $10,500 − $1,200 = $24,300

Debt service (mortgage payments) are not subtracted as an expense.

Math Review

The State of Florida expects its real estate sales associates and brokers to be able to do basic math as it relates to the real estate business. For the most part, this is middle-school- and high-school-level math: word problems using basic calculations (addition, subtraction, multiplication, and division) with a real estate twist. But math is math and for many people it's an intimidating subject.

If you want to brush up on your math skills, you can use this appendix, which is a review of some of the basic math you're expected to know and may be tested on. Nothing beats practice when you're trying to learn math. So after you've reviewed these sample problems, if you feel you need more work, have someone you know make up different problems based on the ones in this section.

My advice is to save all the math problems for the end of the test. You have 3 hours and 30 minutes to complete the exam, so you should have plenty of time to go back and do the math problems. Math problems take longer to compute, so why use precious time up front when you can get all the other questions done first? The bottom line: You could literally skip all the math problems and still pass the exam. The state test for sales associate has ten math questions; the broker test has five math questions. (In addition, the broker exam has five 2-point questions related to a closing problem.)

That said, remember to read the math questions carefully. Make sure you do all the steps. Do them twice if you have time. And relax. Even if you find the math a little difficult, you can still do well on the exam by focusing on the other areas. After a few months as a real estate agent, you'll be able to calculate your commission down to the nearest penny in your head.

Percentages

Many real estate calculations are based on percentages. Perhaps most important of all, the calculation of a commission and its splits with other brokers and sales associates are based on percentages. Also, when two or more people own unequal shares of property, percentages may be used to calculate the value of each share. Valuation calculations may also use percentages when comparing one property to another.

Whether you use a calculator or do problems with pencil and paper, you'll always need to convert a percentage to a decimal number. There are two ways to do this:

- You can divide the percent by 100.
- You can move the decimal point two places to the left. If you choose this method, always remember that, in a whole number, the decimal is usually not shown but is implied at the end of the number.

Whichever method you use here are some examples of what you'll get:

$$7\% = 0.07$$
$$23\% = 0.23$$
$$5.6\% = 0.056$$
$$120\% = 1.20$$

One other thing to remember is that, in order to convert a fraction to a decimal, you divide the *denominator* (the bottom number in a fraction) into the *numerator* (the top number in a fraction). For example ¼ becomes $1 \div 4 = 0.25$. Basic percentage calculations are pretty straightforward.

> **Example 1:** If Owner A owns a 60% share of a building worth $500,000, how much is Owner A's share worth?
> $$\$500,000 \times 0.60 = \$300,000$$

Commission problems are done the same way.

> **Example 2:** What is the commission on a $200,000 sale if the commission rate is 6%?
> $200,000 × 0.06 = $12,000

A variation on the commission problem has to do with how much the owner receives after paying the commission, sometimes called *net to owner.*

> **Example 3:** Suppose you sell a property for $100,000 at a 5% commission. How much does the owner receive after the transaction?
> $100,000 (Sale Price) × 0.05 (Commission Rate) = $5,000 (Commission)
> $100,000 (Sale Price) – $5,000 (Commission) = $95,000 (Net to Owner)

Now suppose we ask the question in a different way.

> **Example 4:** After paying a 5% commission, the owner wants to net $95,000. What should the sale price of the property be?

The easiest thing to do is to add 5% to the $95,000, right? Wrong! Here's the proof that it's wrong:

> $95,000 (Net to Owner) × 0.05 (Commission Rate) = $4,750 (Commission)
> $95,000 (Net to Owner) + $4,750 (Commission) = $99,750 (Sale Price)

Because the owner wants $95,000 net after paying your commission, you'll have to settle for $4,750 rather than $5,000. So how do you do this calculation? Here's the formula:

> Net to Owner ÷ (100% – Commission Rate) = Sale Price

Using the numbers in Example 4:

> $95,000 ÷ (100% – 5%) = Sale Price
> $95,000 ÷ 0.95 = $100,000

You would need to sell the house for $100,000 to have a net to owner of $95,000. Note that I changed 95% to the decimal of 0.95 by moving the decimal point two places to the left (or doing 95 ÷ 100).

Here are some different numbers to show a variation of this method in case you run into it on the exam:

> **Example 5:** You receive a $7,000 commission, which is 4% of the selling price. What did the property sell for?

The formula in this case is:

> Commission (in dollars) ÷ Commission Rate = Sale Price
> $7,000 ÷ 0.04 = $175,000

Note: All commission rates in this section are made up for illustrative purposes only.

Area and Volume

Some basic calculations you need to know have to do with finding the area and volume of various figures. This will also require some knowledge of units of measure.

Sometimes test writers will ask for answers in different units requiring conversion. You'll want to memorize the following common conversion factors:

- **To convert inches to feet,** divide by 12 inches.
- **To convert feet to yards,** divide by 3 feet.
- **To convert feet to miles,** divide by 5,280 feet.
- **To convert square feet to acres,** divide by 43,560 square feet (ft^2).
- **To convert square feet to square yards,** divide by 9 square feet (ft^2).
- **To convert cubic feet to cubic yards,** divide by 27 cubic feet (ft^3).

Area of a Square or Rectangle

The basic formula for both of these calculations is

Area = Length × Width

The units must be the same (yards × yards, feet × feet, inches × inches, and so on). And the answer will always be in square units of the unit you're using.

Be cautious on the exam: Sometimes the test writers will list the right numbers but show them as yards, feet, or inches instead of *square* yards, feet, or inches.

Example 1: What is the area of a square where each side measures 40 feet?

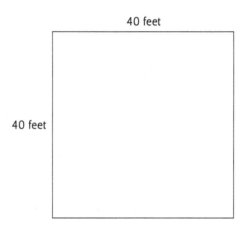

Area = 40 feet × 40 feet = 1,600 square feet

Example 2: What is the area of a rectangle that measures 30 feet by 50 feet?

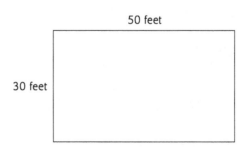

Area = 30 feet × 50 feet = 1,500 square feet

Area of a Triangle

The basic formula for the area of a triangle is

Area = ½ × Base × Height

You may have learned this in school as

Area = (Base × Height) ÷ 2

Either formula works.

Remember when using a calculator that 0.5 is the decimal equivalent of the fraction ½.

Example 1: What is the area of a triangle whose base is 30 feet and whose height is 15 feet?

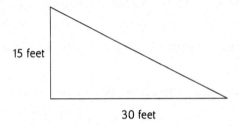

Area = 0.5 × 30 feet × 15 feet = 225 square feet

Example 2: What is the area of the following figure?

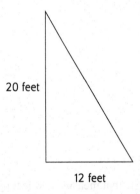

Area = 0.5 × 12 feet × 20 feet = 120 square feet

Area of an Irregular Shape

Many houses are not perfect squares or rectangles. The standard way to deal with calculating the area of an irregularly shaped figure is to divide it into squares, rectangles, and triangles as necessary; then calculate the area of each of the separate figures and add them up to get the total area.

Volume of a Cube or Rectangular Solid

When you add a third dimension to a square or a rectangle, you get a cube or a rectangular solid, respectively. Calculating the volume of a cube or rectangular solid is a matter of placing a third number, usually referred to as the *height,* into the basic area formula (see the "Area of a Square or Rectangle" section earlier):

Volume = Length × Width × Height

Remember: All the units of measure should be the same. The answer will be in cubic units.

Example 1: What is the volume of a room measuring 10 feet long by 10 feet wide, with 10-foot ceilings?

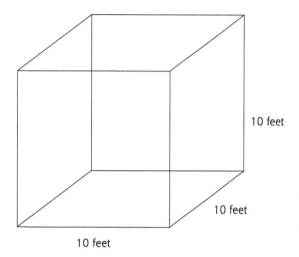

In this example, the 10-foot ceilings are the height of the room, so the formula would look like this:

Volume = 10 feet × 10 feet × 10 feet = 1,000 cubic feet

Example 2: What is the volume of a room measuring 20 feet long by 15 feet wide, with 9-foot ceilings?

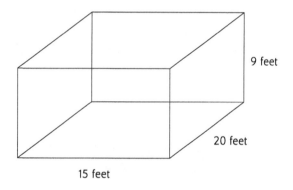

Volume = 20 feet × 15 feet × 9 feet = 2,700 cubic feet

Example 3: What is the volume of a concrete slab patio that is 30 feet long by 20 feet wide by 3 inches deep?

Remember: You must convert the inches to a portion of a foot to use the formula Volume = Length × Width × Height. (See the conversion formulas earlier in this appendix for reference.)

Volume = 30 feet × 20 feet × (3 ÷ 12)
Volume = 30 feet × 20 feet × 0.25 feet = 150 cubic feet

Hint: Don't convert everything to inches. The numbers get too big to work with.

Volume of a Three-Dimensional Triangular Figure or a Pyramid

In real estate, you're likely to encounter three-dimensional triangular figures or pyramids when you're dealing with roofs and attic spaces. A *front-gabled* or *side-gabled roof* is a three-dimensional triangular figure—it has a roofline, and it's the most common kind of roof. You may also find a *hipped roof,* which is shaped like a pyramid.

Here's what a three-dimensional triangular figure looks like:

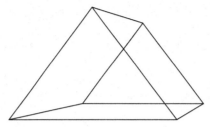

And here's the formula for the volume of this kind of figure:

Volume = Area of Triangular Base × Length

Remember that the area of a triangle is ½ × Base × Height. The tricky part about this type of figure when you're dealing with a roof is that the figure is on its side.

Example 1: Find the volume of an attic that's 20 feet wide by 25 feet long with a roof peak that's 10 feet high.

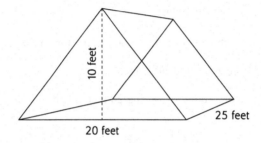

Volume = (½ × 20 feet × 10 feet) × 25 feet = 2,500 cubic feet

A pyramid looks like this:

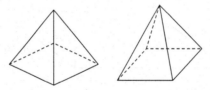

And here's the formula for the volume of a pyramid:

Volume = ⅓ × Area of the Base × Height

Remember that the area of the base is Length × Width.

Example 2: Find the volume of an attic that's 30 feet long by 25 feet wide with a peak that's 15 feet high.

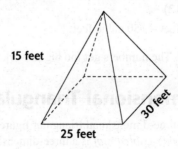

Volume = ⅓ × (25 feet × 30 feet) × 15 feet = 3,750 cubic feet

Mortgage Calculations

Several types of mortgage calculation questions appear on the exam. Here are some examples:

Example 1: What is the first year's interest on a mortgage for $200,000 at 6% interest for 30 years?

Unless otherwise stated, interest is always assumed to be annual. For this type of question, the entire balance is considered to be outstanding in the first year (or an interest-only loan). The term of the mortgage doesn't matter.

$200,000 (Amount of Mortgage) × 0.06 (Interest Rate) = $12,000 (Interest Due the First Year)

Example 2: Using the figures in the previous example, if the loan is an amortized loan, how much interest is due the first month?

$12,000 (First Year's Interest) ÷ 12 months = $1,000 (Interest Due the First Month)

Example 3: Using the information in the previous example, assuming that the monthly *payment* is $1,300, what is the balance owed on the mortgage after the first month's payment is made?

$1,300 (Total Payment) − $1,000 (Interest) = $300 (Principal Paid)

$200,000 (Original Mortgage Amount) − $300 (First Month's Principal Payment) = $199,700 (Balance)

Remember: In an amortized mortgage, each payment is made up of principal and interest.

Another common mortgage question asks you to calculate the amount necessary to *amortize* (or pay off) a certain amount of mortgage at a certain interest rate for a certain term given a monthly payment of a certain amount per $1,000 of mortgage.

Example 4: A 20-year mortgage at 5½% carries a monthly payment of $6.60 per thousand. What is the total monthly payment for a $275,000 mortgage?

$275,000 ÷ $1,000 = 275 units of $1,000 each

275 × $6.60 (Payment per Thousand) = $1,815 per month

Proration

Proration problems are sometimes asked on real estate exams whether it is common in your area to close title through an escrow agent or in a face-to-face closing. The theory of proration is quite simple, and understanding the theory helps you understand the math.

Taxes (or any other costs such as homeowners' association fees) are paid either in advance or in arrears for a certain period of time. In Florida, taxes are paid in arrears in November for the entire year that is just ending. This means that the owner has used the property before he has paid the taxes for that period of use. *Proration* is simply reconciling the payment with the period of time that the property was used. Florida uses a 365-day year to divide the taxes between the buyer and seller, and the buyer is charged for the taxes on the day of closing.

Example 1: Taxes of $1,788.50 are paid in arrears on November 10 for the year. Closing occurs on December 10. What is the tax proration?

$1,800 ÷ 365 days = $4.90 per day

Counting from the date of closing, the new owner will own the house for 22 days and, therefore, she'll owe the seller 22 days' worth of taxes.

2 days × $4.90 /day = $107.80

In proration terminology, the seller gets a credit of $107.80 and the buyer gets a debit of $107.80.

Example 2: Let's say homeowners' association fees are paid in advance at the beginning of the month. To keep it simple, we'll say that they are $300 and the closing on the property is June 20 (June is a 30-day month). Assuming that the buyer is charged for the day of closing, who owes how much to whom?

$300 ÷ 30 days = $10 per day

The seller has already paid the full amount, but the buyer will own the property for 11 days.

11 days × $10 per day = $110 (Amount the Buyer Owes the Seller)

Note: For exam purposes, the terms *tax year* and *fiscal year* may be used interchangeably.

Appraisal and Valuation

Appraisal and valuation are extremely complex subjects, but there are some basic mathematical formulas that examiners expect you to be able to handle. In general, the formulas deal with the income approach to appraising commercial properties. The basic formulas and their variations follow.

Capitalization

Income ÷ Capitalization Rate = Value

Income ÷ Value = Capitalization Rate

Capitalization Rate × Value = Income

Income refers to *net operating income,* which is income after certain expenses have been deducted. The *capitalization rate* is often referred to as the *rate of return. Property value* is the same as the sale price when this formula is used.

Example 1: Calculate the value of a building whose net operating income is $32,000 when the capitalization rate is 8%.

$32,000 ÷ 0.08 = $400,000

Example 2: Calculate the capitalization rate of a building that sold for $720,000 with an income of $90,000.

$90,000 ÷ $720,000 = 0.125 or 12.5%

Example 3: What is the income of a building that you paid $650,000 for at a rate of return of 7%?

$650,000 × 0.07 = $45,000

Remember: All the numbers in these formulas are annual. If you're given a monthly income, you have to first multiply it by 12.

Note: When doing calculations on your calculator, you might get something like 166.66666666. Rounding to two places past the decimal is pretty typical. In some exams, the test writer will round the answer to a whole number (which in the case of 166.66666666 would be 167). I suggest that if you can set the decimal places on your calculator, you set it for three places after the decimal place. Test writers will usually not provide answers that are so close that rounding could make a difference between selecting the right or wrong answer. But you should be prepared for any possibility, like the following:

Assuming the total value of the property to be $190,000 and the total net income to be $13,680, what would be the capitalization rate?

A. 6.5%
B. 7%
C. 7.2%
D. 7.5%

Here, if your calculator is set to use a floating decimal or automatically rounds off to two decimal places, the answer will come up as 0.07, which you would take to be 7% (Choice B), when the correct answer is actually 0.072, or 7.2% (Choice C).

Gross Multipliers

Another way that value is calculated uses multipliers to convert income into value.

The gross income multiplier (GIM) is usually based on annual income. The gross rent multiplier (GRM) is based on monthly income. The formulas are the same regardless of which multiplier is used. You only need to make sure you use annual or monthly rent appropriately.

Income × GRM = Value

Value ÷ Income = GRM

Value ÷ GRM = Income

For purposes of these formulas, sale price and value are considered to be the same.

Example 1: A property has a gross monthly income of $3,000. Properties in this area of this type are selling at a GRM of 120. What is the value of the property?

$3,000 × 120 = $360,000

Example 2: A property has an annual income of $35,000. It sold for $700,000. What is its GIM?

$700,000 ÷ $35,000 = 20

Remember: GIMs use annual numbers.

Example 3: A property that is valued at $550,000 sells at a GRM of 110. What is its monthly income?

$550,000 ÷ 110 = $5,000 per month

Notes

Notes

Notes

Notes

Notes

Notes

Notes

Notes